Third Edition

GREAT JOBS

FOR

Liberal Arts
Majors

W9-BVE-598

Blythe Camenson

New York Chicago San Francisco Lisbon London Madrid Mexico City
Milan New Delhi San Juan Seoul Singapore Sydney Toronto

Library of Congress Cataloging-in-Publication Data

Camenson, Blythe.
   Great jobs for liberal arts majors / by Blythe Camenson—3rd ed.
       p. cm.
   Includes index.
   ISBN 0-07-148214-8 (alk. paper)
   1. Vocational guidance—United States. 2. College graduates—Employment—United States.
   3. Bachelor of arts degree—United States. 4. Master of arts degree—United States. I. Title.
   HF5382.5.U5C252 2008
   331.702′35—dc22   2007010794

1 2 3 4 5 6 7 8 9 10 11 12 13 14 15 16 17 18 19 20 21 22 23   DOC/DOC   0 9 8 7

ISBN 978-0-07-148214-1
MHID   0-07-148214-8

McGraw-Hill books are available at special quantity discounts to use as premiums and sales promotions, or for use in corporate training programs. For more information, please write to the Director of Special Sales, Professional Publishing, McGraw-Hill, Two Penn Plaza, New York, NY 10121-2298. Or contact your local bookstore.

This book is printed on acid-free paper.

To all my professors at the University of Massachusetts, Boston, who guided me carefully down the path of a liberal arts education.

Contents

Acknowledgments

The author wishes to thank Josephine Scanlon for her assistance in revising this edition.

Introduction: Investigate the Opportunities

As a liberal arts major, you've probably heard more than one person comment that while you might graduate with a well-rounded education, you'll probably find it difficult to get a good job—unless, of course, you plan to teach. While teaching is a perfectly fine goal for many liberal arts majors, it is often assumed to be the only thing that you'll be qualified for with a degree in English, philosophy, sociology, French, women's studies, or the scores of other majors that fall into the liberal arts category.

Like many students before you, you might be progressing through your liberal arts program, semester after semester, year after year, taking your major courses, and signing up for your electives, but you're not really sure where you'll be the day after graduation. Maybe some friends or family members have advised you that if you want to have a successful career, you should be majoring in a professional area, such as engineering, accounting, or nursing. They believe that this will almost guarantee you a good job. And it well might, but those professional programs aren't for you. You don't want to graduate with specific knowledge of only one field and then learn that you don't really enjoy the work.

So what in the world will you be able to do with that B.A. in psychology, math, Russian history, German literature, or political science? Have you been wasting your time? Will you graduate with nothing more than the ability to entertain party guests with conversation on a variety of interesting and socially relevant topics? And how will you even be able to throw a party without an income? One thing you know for sure: intelligent conversation does not pay the bills.

Now is the time to put all those fears aside. With some advanced planning and an acquired understanding of your options, you will find that your career choices are as diverse as the number of liberal arts majors—maybe even more so. While it's true that nursing majors become nurses and accounting majors become accountants, an English or philosophy major has many more career options than teaching.

Advice from the Experts

Listen to what a professional in the area has to say. Marcia Harris is coauthor of *The Parent's Crash Course in Career Planning*, as well as the director of University Career Services at the University of North Carolina at Chapel Hill.

"We are strong proponents of liberal arts degrees at the university," she says. "We think liberal arts gives students the broadest background in communication skills, reasoning ability, and the ability to learn.

"It's true that sometimes employers, especially the first-line hiring managers, tend to be a little short-sighted when it comes to liberal arts skills. They think they want recent graduates who can 'hit the ground running.' But there have been a number of research studies to support the fact that the higher up you go—to the higher-level managers and CEOs—the more these people appreciate the value of a liberal arts degree and look for job candidates who have those broad-based skills.

"It's sort of a good news–bad news situation. It's harder for liberal arts graduates to find a job initially, but in the long run, that degree serves them really well.

"What we try to do to is help our students have the best of both worlds, putting the emphasis on skills as opposed to college major. We also try to reach them as early as freshman or sophomore year and say to them, 'You can prepare to enter most career fields with a liberal arts degree, but the degree alone is not going to open the doors. If you want to be a banker, for example, you don't have to be a business major, you could be a philosophy major. However, you'll need to demonstrate to the bank executive whom you interview with during your senior year that you can handle quantitative skills and have a legitimate interest in business.'

"A judicious use of electives, part-time work, and internships in related fields is critical. Involvement with campus organizations is also invaluable. For example, on our campus we have more than three hundred different organizations, such as the investment club, the entrepreneur club, and the business students' association. You don't have to be a business major to belong. If you're a student majoring in political science but thinking about going into advertising, you can join some of these organizations and acquire leadership roles over a period of years. You are really building your portfolio to make your case to an employer. You can say, 'I wanted to get this broad-based education, but I have some skills that you might be interested in that relate to this particular position.'"

Here are what some other people have to say on the subject. They are not career counselors or student advisers, but professionals out in the workforce who started their education with a liberal arts degree.

Marshall J. Cook is an author and a professor at the University of Wisconsin, Madison. He says, "A liberal arts degree prepares you to think. It prepares you to deal with complexity, ambiguity, and contradiction. It helps you distinguish among conflicting points of view and broadens your perspective on life.

"Because it does all that, a liberal arts degree is a wonderful preparation for life and for the world of work, in all its complexity, ambiguity, and contradiction.

"Sometimes graduate school is necessary. I went because I wasn't ready for a 'career' and didn't know what I wanted to do. I've never been sorry. A master's degree opened up many doors for me, including the job I have now as a professor in an adult education communications department. If the job you want requires it, if you feel you have more to learn in a structured learning setting, and if you can afford the time and money, go for it." (See Marshall Cook's firsthand account in Chapter 6.)

Betsy Lancefield Lane is an editor. "I really wanted the old-fashioned, well-rounded education," she says. "I didn't want to know just one subject area. I wanted to be conversant in many different areas. In addition, to be honest, I didn't like any one area enough to do only that. I have a B.A. in general studies with an emphasis in linguistics. At the time I graduated, there was a lot of emphasis on the business world. They wanted people who knew how to think, who could write, and who had a diverse knowledge and skills base. You end up with terrific versatility.

"The criticism of such a broad major, of course, is that you haven't really specialized in anything. That could be a valid criticism, but often employers will say that they'll train you to perform the tasks they need. What they want is candidates with a basic literacy and ability to solve problems, think creatively, and communicate with people. As far as the particular skills you'll need for the job, they'll train you.

"I think my job as an editor is a great job for a liberal arts major. I use the writing skills I got in college, and my familiarity with a broad spectrum of subjects is very helpful. Right now the books I edit are about careers, an area I've mostly learned about on the job. But if I started working with, say, history books, then I'd draw on the information I learned in my history courses. Or I could work on literature books and have a baseline familiarity with that material.

"I feel that the liberal arts degree has allowed me to get started on a lot of diverse projects. The subject areas aren't completely foreign to me."

Gerald D. Oster, a clinical psychologist, says, "If you think of learning as a lifelong process, a liberal arts education starts you along this path. You gain broad exposure to history, social systems, art, and culture; you learn to assimilate new possibilities for yourself. You also learn to think and communicate critically, examining others' works with a critical mind, instead of depending on others to interpret things for you.

"You prepare yourself for the adult world of work, family, and community service by gaining deeper appreciation for a variety of areas. You begin to see the world through a larger framework, which can change and define your own likes and dislikes.

"A liberal arts education is broad-based but essential in many forms of work. The workforce is filled with more than just technocrats or specialists. Even these highly trained people need to understand and communicate their efforts to the rest of the world and appreciate their accomplishments within the context of everyday people. The world is vast and interesting for you to explore, and a broad-based education allows you that comfort in many arenas." (See Chapter 10 for a closer look at Gerald Oster's job.)

The Road Ahead

In Part One of this book you will learn many valuable tips on the job search, with emphasis on conducting a self-assessment, preparing a résumé and cover letter, researching careers, and interviewing and considering job offers.

In Part Two, you will explore a variety of career paths, many that are open to any liberal arts majors, some that are more defined, and still some that require further education or training. Chapter Five will give you a broad overview of the various paths; the remaining chapters will help you narrow those paths.

Once you've found the path you want to follow, you'll realize how important your liberal arts degree is in reaching your ultimate destination.

PART ONE

THE JOB SEARCH

I

The Self-Assessment

Self-assessment is the process by which you begin to acknowledge your own particular blend of education, experiences, values, needs, and goals. It provides the foundation for career planning and the entire job search process. Self-assessment involves looking inward and asking yourself what can sometimes prove to be difficult questions. This self-examination should lead to an intimate understanding of your personal traits and values, consumption patterns and economic needs, longer-term goals, skill base, preferred skills, and underdeveloped skills.

You come to the self-assessment process knowing yourself well in some of these areas, but you may still be uncertain about other aspects. You may be well aware of your consumption patterns, but have you spent much time specifically identifying your longer-term goals or your personal values as they relate to work? No matter what level of self-assessment you have undertaken to date, it is now time to clarify all of these issues and questions as they relate to the job search.

The knowledge you gain in the self-assessment process will guide the rest of your job search. In this book, you will learn about all of the following tasks:

- Writing résumés and cover letters
- Researching careers and networking
- Interviewing and job offer considerations

In each of these steps, you will rely on and often return to the understanding gained through your self-assessment. Any individual seeking employment must be able and willing to express these facets of his or her personality to recruiters and interviewers throughout the job search. This communication allows you to show the world who you are so that together with employers you can determine whether there will be a workable match with a given job or career path.

How to Conduct a Self-Assessment

The self-assessment process goes on naturally all the time. People ask you to clarify what you mean, you make a purchasing decision, or you begin a new relationship. You react to the world and the world reacts to you. How you understand these interactions and any changes you might make because of them are part of the natural process of self-discovery. There is, however, a more comprehensive and efficient way to approach self-assessment with regard to employment.

Because self-assessment can become a complex exercise, we have distilled it into a seven-step process that provides an effective basis for undertaking a job search. The seven steps include the following:

1. Understanding your personal traits
2. Identifying your personal values
3. Calculating your economic needs
4. Exploring your longer-term goals
5. Enumerating your skill base
6. Recognizing your preferred skills
7. Assessing skills needing further development

As you work through your self-assessment, you might want to create a worksheet similar to the one shown in Exhibit 1.1, starting on the following page. Or you might want to keep a journal of the thoughts you have as you undergo this process. There will be many opportunities to revise your self-assessment as you start down the path of seeking a career.

Step 1   Understand Your Personal Traits
Each person has a unique personality that he or she brings to the job search process. Gaining a better understanding of your personal traits can help you evaluate job and career choices. Identifying these traits and then finding employment that allows you to draw on at least some of them can create a rewarding and fulfilling work experience. If potential employment doesn't allow you to use these preferred traits, it is important to decide whether you

Exhibit 1.1
SELF-ASSESSMENT WORKSHEET

Step 1. Understand Your Personal Traits

The personal traits that describe me are
(Include all of the words that describe you.)
The ten personal traits that most accurately describe me are
(List these ten traits.)

Step 2. Identify Your Personal Values

Working conditions that are important to me include
(List working conditions that would have to exist for you to accept a position.)
The values that go along with my working conditions are
(Write down the values that correspond to each working condition.)
Some additional values I've decided to include are
(List those values you identify as you conduct this job search.)

Step 3. Calculate Your Economic Needs

My estimated minimum annual salary requirement is
(Write the salary you have calculated based on your budget.)
Starting salaries for the positions I'm considering are
(List the name of each job you are considering and the associated starting salary.)

Step 4. Explore Your Longer-Term Goals

My thoughts on longer-term goals right now are
(Jot down some of your longer-term goals as you know them right now.)

Step 5. Enumerate Your Skill Base

The general skills I possess are
(List the skills that underlie tasks you are able to complete.)
The specific skills I possess are
(List more technical or specific skills that you possess, and indicate your level of expertise.)
General and specific skills that I want to promote to employers for the jobs I'm considering are
(List general and specific skills for each type of job you are considering.)

continued

Step 6. Recognize Your Preferred Skills

Skills that I would like to use on the job include

(List skills that you hope to use on the job, and indicate how often you'd like to use them.)

Step 7. Assess Skills Needing Further Development

Some skills that I'll need to acquire for the jobs I'm considering include

(Write down skills listed in job advertisements or job descriptions that you don't currently possess.)

I believe I can build these skills by

(Describe how you plan to acquire these skills.)

---

can find other ways to express them or whether you would be better off not considering this type of job. Interests and hobbies pursued outside of work hours can be one way to use personal traits you don't have an opportunity to draw on in your work. For example, if you consider yourself an outgoing person and the kinds of jobs you are examining allow little contact with other people, you may be able to achieve the level of interaction that is comfortable for you outside of your work setting. If such a compromise seems impractical or otherwise unsatisfactory, you probably should explore only jobs that provide the interaction you want and need on the job.

Many young adults who are not very confident about their employability will downplay their need for income. They will say, "Money is not all that important if I love my work." But if you begin to document exactly what you need for housing, transportation, insurance, clothing, food, and utilities, you will begin to understand that some jobs cannot meet your financial needs and it doesn't matter how wonderful the job is. If you have to worry each payday about bills and other financial obligations, you won't be very effective on the job. Begin now to be honest with yourself about your needs.

Begin the self-assessment process by creating an inventory of your personal traits. Make a list of as many words as possible to describe yourself. Words like *accurate, creative, future-oriented, relaxed,* or *structured* are just a few examples. In addition, you might ask people who know you well how they might describe you.

Focus on Selected Personal Traits. Of all the traits you identified, select the ten you believe most accurately describe you. Keep track of these ten traits.

Consider Your Personal Traits in the Job Search Process. As you begin exploring jobs and careers, watch for matches between your personal traits and the job descriptions you read. Some jobs will require many personal traits you know you possess, and others will not seem to match those traits.

For example, compare the jobs of the in-house editor and a freelance writer. The job of an editor, for example, requires observation skills, attention to detail, and the ability to work under pressure as part of a team. Editors often handle several projects simultaneously, and they must be able to work with strict deadlines and adapt to last-minute changes. They also must be able to manage staff and coordinate others' work to make sure that schedules are adhered to. A freelance writer who provides stories to the newspaper, on the other hand, most likely works alone, while conducting research and writing articles. Although both in-house editor and freelancer writer must be able to manage their time and meet deadlines, the freelancer generally has less interaction with others and must be able to work independently.

Your ability to respond to changing conditions, your decision-making ability, productivity, creativity, and verbal skills all have a bearing on your success in and enjoyment of your work life. To better guarantee success, be sure to take the time needed to understand these traits in yourself.

Step 2 Identify Your Personal Values

Your personal values affect every aspect of your life, including employment, and they develop and change as you move through life. Values can be defined as principles that we hold in high regard, qualities that are important and desirable to us. Some values aren't ordinarily connected to work (love, beauty, color, light, relationships, family, or religion), and others are (autonomy, cooperation, effectiveness, achievement, knowledge, and security). Our values determine, in part, the level of satisfaction we feel in a particular job.

Define Acceptable Working Conditions. One facet of employment is the set of working conditions that must exist for someone to consider taking a job.

Each of us would probably create a unique list of acceptable working conditions, but items that might be included on many people's lists are the amount of money you would need to be paid, how far you are willing to drive or travel, the amount of freedom you want in determining your own schedule, whether you would be working with people or data or things, and the types of tasks you would be willing to do. Your conditions might include statements of working conditions you will *not* accept; for example, you might not be willing to work at night or on weekends or holidays.

If you were offered a job tomorrow, what conditions would have to exist for you to realistically consider accepting the position? Take some time and make a list of these conditions.

Realize Associated Values. Your list of working conditions can be used to create an inventory of your values relating to jobs and careers you are exploring. For example, if one of your conditions stated that you wanted to earn at least $30,000 per year, the associated value would be financial gain. If another condition was that you wanted to work with a friendly group of people, the value that went along with that might be belonging or interaction with people.

Relate Your Values to the World of Work. As you read the job descriptions you come across either in this book, in newspapers and magazines, or online, think about the values associated with each position.

For example, the duties of a freelance magazine writer include finding topics, researching stories, and writing material that suits the requirements of the publication. Associated values are creativity, independence, and intellectual stimulation.

At least some of the associated values in the field you're exploring should match those you extracted from your list of working conditions. Take a second look at any values that don't match up. How important are they to you? What will happen if they are not satisfied on the job? Can you incorporate those personal values elsewhere? Your answers need to be brutally honest. As you continue your exploration, be sure to add to your list any additional values that occur to you.

Step 3   Calculate Your Economic Needs

Each of us grew up in an environment that provided for certain basic needs, such as food and shelter, and, to varying degrees, other needs that we now consider basic, such as cable television, e-mail, or an automobile. Needs such as privacy, space, and quiet, which at first glance may not appear to be monetary needs, may add to housing expenses and so should be considered as you examine your economic needs. For example, if you place a high value on a large, open living space for yourself, it would be difficult to satisfy that need without an associated high housing cost, especially in a densely populated city environment.

As you prepare to move into the world of work and become responsible for meeting your own basic needs, it is important to consider the salary you will need to be able to afford a satisfying standard of living. The three-step process outlined here will help you plan a budget, which in turn will allow you to evaluate the various career choices and geographic locations you are considering. The steps include (1) develop a realistic budget, (2) examine starting salaries, and (3) use a cost-of-living index.

Develop a Realistic Budget. Each of us has certain expectations for the kind of lifestyle we want to maintain. To begin the process of defining your economic needs, it will be helpful to determine what you expect to spend on routine monthly expenses. These expenses include housing, food, transportation, entertainment, utilities, loan repayments, and revolving charge accounts. You may not currently spend anything for certain items, but you probably will have to once you begin supporting yourself. As you develop this budget, be generous in your estimates, but keep in mind any items that could be reduced or eliminated. If you are not sure about the cost of a certain item, talk with family or friends who would be able to give you a realistic estimate.

If this is new or difficult for you, start to keep a log of expenses right now. You may be surprised at how much you actually spend each month for food or stamps or magazines. Household expenses and personal grooming items can often loom very large in a budget, as can auto repairs or home maintenance.

Income taxes must also be taken into consideration when examining salary requirements. State and local taxes vary, so it is difficult to calculate exactly the effect of taxes on the amount of income you need to generate. To roughly estimate the gross income necessary to generate your minimum annual salary requirement, multiply the minimum salary you have calculated by a factor of 1.35. The resulting figure will be an approximation of what your gross income would need to be, given your estimated expenses.

Examine Starting Salaries. Starting salaries for each of the career tracks are provided throughout this book. These salary figures can be used in conjunction with the cost-of-living index (discussed in the next section) to determine whether you would be able to meet your basic economic needs in a given geographic location.

Use a Cost-of-Living Index. If you are thinking about trying to get a job in a geographic region other than the one where you now live, understanding differences in the cost of living will help you come to a more informed decision about making a move. By using a cost-of-living index, you can compare salaries offered and the cost of living in different locations with what you know about the salaries offered and the cost of living in your present location.

Many variables are used to calculate the cost-of-living index. Often included are housing, groceries, utilities, transportation, health care, clothing, and entertainment expenses. Right now you do not need to worry about the details associated with calculating a given index. The main purpose of this exercise is to help you understand that pay ranges for entry-level positions may not vary greatly, but the cost of living in different locations *can* vary tremendously.

Imagine that you live in Philadelphia, Pennsylvania, where you earn $50,440 as a public relations specialist. You're thinking of relocating and are considering positions in both Memphis, Tennessee, and San Francisco, California. You know that you can live on $50,440 in Philadelphia, but will this salary be enough to support you in either Memphis or San Francisco? Figuring out the cost-of-living index for each city will show you how much you need to earn to live there comfortably.

In a cost-of-living index, the number 100 represents the national average cost of living, and each city is assigned an index number based on current prices in that city for the items included in the index (housing, food, insurance, etc.). These indices change constantly based on fluctuations in costs around the country.

In this example, Philadelphia's index is 119.0, Memphis's is 89.9, and San Francisco's is 177.0. You can see that it costs nearly twice as much to live in San Francisco as in Memphis, which costs less than Philadelphia. The following table shows how much you would have to earn in both Memphis and San Francisco to maintain the same lifestyle that you have in Philadelphia.

Job: Public Relations Specialist

City	Index	Equivalent Salary
Philadelphia	119.0	
Memphis	89.9	$\frac{119.0}{89.9} \times \$50,440 = \$38,773$ in Memphis
Philadelphia	119.0	
San Francisco	177.0	$\frac{119.0}{177.0} \times \$50,440 = \$67,895$ in San Francisco

This means that you'll have to earn over $17,000 more to maintain the same lifestyle in San Francisco that you have in Philadelphia. On the other hand, you could save money by moving to Memphis, where a salary of $50,440 would leave you with nearly $12,000 in extra money, based on that city's cost-of-living index.

You don't have to do the math yourself. Typing "salary conversion" or "salary calculator" into a search engine will give you plenty of free options.

You can work through a similar exercise for any type of job you are considering and for many locations when current salary information is available. It will be worth your time to undertake this analysis if you are seriously considering a relocation. By doing so you will be able to make an informed choice.

Step 4   Explore Your Longer-Term Goals

There is no question that when we first begin working, our goals are to use our skills and education in a job that will reward us with employment, income, and status relative to the preparation we brought with us to this position. If we are not being paid as much as we feel we should for our level of education or if job demands don't provide the intellectual stimulation we had hoped for, we experience unhappiness and as a result often seek other employment.

Most jobs we consider "good" are those that fulfill our basic "lower-level" needs of security, food, clothing, shelter, income, and productive work. But even when our basic needs are met and our jobs are secure and productive, we as individuals are constantly changing. As we change, the demands and expectations we place on our jobs may change. Fortunately, some jobs grow and change with us, and this explains why some people are happy throughout many years in a job.

But more often people are bigger than the jobs they fill. We have more goals and needs than any job could satisfy. These are "higher-level" needs of self-esteem, companionship, affection, and an increasing desire to feel we are employing ourselves in the most effective way possible. Not all of these higher-level needs can be met through employment, but for as long as we are employed, we increasingly demand that our jobs play their part in moving us along the path to fulfillment.

Another obvious but important fact is that we change as we mature. Although our jobs also have the potential for change, they may not change as frequently or as markedly as we do. There are increasingly fewer one-job, one-employer careers; we must think about a work future that may involve voluntary or forced moves from employer to employer. Because of that very real possibility, we need to take advantage of the opportunities in each position we hold. Acquiring the skills and competencies associated with each position will keep us viable and attractive as employees. This is particularly true in a job market that not only is technology/computer dependent, but also is populated with more and more small, self-transforming organizations rather than the large, seemingly stable organizations of the past.

If you are considering a career as a public relations specialist, you might gain a better perspective on the job by talking with people who are employed in different types of public relations work. For instance, talking with public relations specialists who work on political campaigns, in health care, and in employee and investor relations will give you insight into different aspects of the work. Ask these people if they will take the time to speak with you, and be prepared with a list of questions.

Step 5   Enumerate Your Skill Base

In terms of the job search, skills can be thought of as capabilities that can be developed in school, at work, or by volunteering and then used in specific job settings. Many studies have documented the kinds of skills that employers seek in entry-level applicants. For example, some of the most desired skills for individuals interested in the teaching profession are the ability to interact effectively with students one-on-one, to manage a classroom, to adapt to varying situations as necessary, and to get involved in school activities. Business employers have also identified important qualities, including enthusiasm for the employer's product or service, a businesslike mind, the ability to follow written or oral instructions, the ability to demonstrate self-control, the confidence to suggest new ideas, the ability to communicate with all members of a group, an awareness of cultural differences, and loyalty, to name just a few. You will find that many of these skills are also in the repertoire of qualities demanded in your college major.

To be successful in obtaining any given job, you must be able to demonstrate that you possess a certain mix of skills that will allow you to carry out the duties required by that job. This skill mix will vary a great deal from job to job; to determine the skills necessary for the jobs you are seeking, you can read job advertisements or more generic job descriptions, such as those found later in this book. If you want to be effective in the job search, you must directly show employers that you possess the skills needed to be successful in filling the position. These skills will initially be described on your résumé and then discussed again during the interview process.

Skills are either general or specific. To develop a list of skills relevant to employers, you must first identify the general skills you possess, then list specific skills you have to offer, and, finally, examine which of these skills employers are seeking.

Identify Your General Skills. Because you possess or will possess a college degree, employers will assume that you can read and write, perform certain basic computations, think critically, and communicate effectively. Employers will want to see that you have acquired these skills, and they will want to know which additional general skills you possess.

One way to begin identifying skills is to write an experiential diary. An experiential diary lists all the tasks you were responsible for completing for each job you've held and then outlines the skills required to do those tasks. You may list several skills for any given task. This diary allows you to distinguish between the tasks you performed and the underlying skills required to complete those tasks. Here's an example:

Tasks	Skills
Answering telephone	Effective use of language, clear diction, ability to direct inquiries, ability to solve problems
Waiting on tables	Poise under conditions of time and pressure, speed, accuracy, good memory, simultaneous completion of tasks, sales skills

For each job or experience you have participated in, develop a worksheet based on the example shown here. On a résumé, you may want to describe these skills rather than simply listing tasks. Skills are easier for the employer to appreciate, especially when your experience is very different from the employment you are seeking. In addition to helping you identify general skills, this experiential diary will prepare you to speak more effectively in an interview about the qualifications you possess.

Identify Your Specific Skills. It may be easier to identify your specific skills because you can definitely say whether you can speak other languages, program a computer, draft a map or diagram, or edit a document using appropriate symbols and terminology.

Using your experiential diary, identify the points in your history where you learned how to do something very specific, and decide whether you have a beginning, intermediate, or advanced knowledge of how to use that particular skill. Right now, be sure to list *every* specific skill you have, and don't consider whether you like using the skill. Write down a list of specific skills you have acquired and the level of competence you possess—beginning, intermediate, or advanced.

Relate Your Skills to Employers. You probably have thought about a couple of different jobs you might be interested in obtaining, and one way to begin relating the general and specific skills you possess to a potential employer's needs is to read actual advertisements for these types of positions (see Part Two for resources listing actual job openings).

Suppose you are interested in a career as a public relations specialist working in the health care field. A typical job listing might read, "Minimum requirements include an M.A. and four years' experience, organizational skills and the ability to work under pressure." You can find additional information about the job of a public relations specialist in health care by using any of a number of general sources of information. For example, public relations specialists in the health field also conduct interviews, write reports, assemble focus groups, and interact with the media.

As you research these additional sources of information, begin to compile a list of required skills. Studying advertisements for related positions will help you determine the core skills you'll need to pursue the work you want to do. Include both general and specific skills. The following is a sample list of skills you would need to work as a public relations specialist in the health care field:

Job: Public Relations Specialist

General Skills	Specific Skills
Organization	Write reports
Communication	Conduct interviews
Creativity	Write press releases
Work as part of a team	Write memos
Pay attention to details	Lead meetings

Once you've assembled this list, take a separate sheet of paper and try generating a comprehensive list of skills required for at least one job you are considering. The list of skills for a given career path will be valuable for a number of jobs because the skills are general. For example, writing press releases is also a required skill for public relations specialists working in politics.

Step 6   Recognize Your Preferred Skills

In the previous section you developed a comprehensive list of skills that relate to particular career paths that are of interest to you. You can now relate these to skills that you prefer to use. We all use a wide range of skills (some researchers say individuals have a repertoire of about five hundred skills), but we may not particularly be interested in using all of them in our work. There may be some skills that come to us more naturally or that we use successfully time and time again and that we want to continue to use; these are best described as our preferred skills. For this exercise use the list of skills that you created for the previous section, and decide which of them you are *most interested in using* in future work and how often you would like to use them. You might be interested in using some skills only occasionally, while others you would like to use more regularly. You probably also have skills that you hope you can use constantly.

As you examine job announcements, look for matches between this list of preferred skills and the qualifications described in the advertisements. These skills should be highlighted on your résumé and discussed in job interviews.

Step 7   Assess Skills Needing Further Development

Previously you compiled a list of general and specific skills required for given positions. You already possess some of these skills; those that remain to be developed are your underdeveloped skills.

If you are just beginning the job search, there may be gaps between the qualifications required for some of the jobs you're considering and the skills you possess. The thought of having to admit to and talk about these underdeveloped skills, especially in a job interview, is a frightening one. One way to put a healthy perspective on this subject is to target and relate your exploration of underdeveloped skills to the types of positions you are seeking. Recognizing these shortcomings and planning to overcome them with either on-the-job training or additional formal education can be a positive way to address the concept of underdeveloped skills.

On your worksheet or in your journal, make a list of up to five general or specific skills required for the positions you're interested in that you *don't currently possess*. For each item list an idea you have for specific action you could take to acquire that skill. Do some brainstorming to come up with possible actions. If you have a hard time generating ideas, talk to people currently working in this type of position, professionals in your college career services office, trusted friends, family members, or members of related professional associations.

In the chapter on interviewing, we will discuss in detail how to effectively address questions about underdeveloped skills. Generally speaking, though, employers want genuine answers to these types of questions. They want you to reveal "the real you," and they also want to see how you answer difficult questions. In taking the positive, targeted approach discussed previously, you show the employer that you are willing to continue to learn and that you have a plan for strengthening your job qualifications.

Use Your Self-Assessment

Exploring entry-level career options can be an exciting experience if you have good resources available and will take the time to use them. Can you effectively complete the following tasks?

1. Understand your personality traits and relate them to career choices
2. Define your personal values
3. Determine your economic needs
4. Explore longer-term goals
5. Understand your skill base
6. Recognize your preferred skills
7. Express a willingness to improve on your underdeveloped skills

If so, then you can more meaningfully participate in the job search process by writing a more effective résumé, finding job titles that represent work you are interested in doing, locating job sites that will provide the opportunity for you to use your strengths and skills, networking in an informed way, participating in focused interviews, getting the most out of follow-up contacts, and evaluating job offers to find those that create a good match between you and the employer. The remaining chapters in Part One guide you through these next steps in the job search process. For many job seekers, this process can take anywhere from three months to a year to implement. The time you will need to put into your job search will depend on the type of job you want and the geographic location where you'd like to work. Think of your effort as a job in itself, requiring you to set aside time each week to complete the needed work. Carefully undertaken efforts may reduce the time you need for your job search.

2

The Résumé and Cover Letter

The task of writing a résumé may seem overwhelming if you are unfamiliar with this type of document, but there are some easily understood techniques that can and should be used. This section was written to help you understand the purpose of the résumé, the different types of formats available, and how to write the sections that contain information traditionally found on a résumé. We will present examples and explanations that address questions frequently posed by people writing their first résumé or updating an old one.

Even within the formats and suggestions given, however, there are infinite variations. True, most follow one of the outlines suggested, but you should feel free to adjust the résumé to suit your needs and make it expressive of your life and experience.

Why Write a Résumé?

The purpose of a résumé is to convince an employer that you should be interviewed. Whether you're mailing, faxing, or e-mailing this document, you'll want to present enough information to show that you can make an immediate and valuable contribution to an organization. A résumé is not an in-depth historical or legal document; later in the job search process you may be asked to document your entire work history on an application form and attest to its validity. The résumé should, instead, highlight relevant information pertaining directly to the organization that will receive the document or to the type of position you are seeking.

We will discuss the chronological and digital résumés in detail here. Functional and targeted résumés, which are used much less often, are briefly discussed. The reasons for using one type of résumé over another and the typical format for each are addressed in the following sections.

The Chronological Résumé

The chronological résumé is the most common of the various résumé formats and therefore the format that employers are most used to receiving. This type of résumé is easy to read and understand because it details the chronological progression of jobs you have held. (See Exhibit 2.1.) It begins with your most recent employment and works back in time. If you have a solid work history or have experience that provided growth and development in your duties and responsibilities, a chronological résumé will highlight these achievements. The typical elements of a chronological résumé include the heading, a career objective, educational background, employment experience, activities, and references.

The Heading
The heading consists of your name, address, telephone number, and other means of contact. This may include a fax number, e-mail address, and your home-page address. If you are using a shared e-mail account or a parent's business fax, be sure to let others who use these systems know that you may receive important professional correspondence via these systems. You wouldn't want to miss a vital e-mail or fax! Likewise, if your résumé directs readers to a personal home page on the Web, be certain it's a professional personal home page designed to be viewed and appreciated by a prospective employer. This may mean making substantial changes in the home page you currently mount on the Web.

The Objective
Without a doubt the objective statement is the most challenging part of the résumé for most writers. Even for individuals who have decided on a career path, it can be difficult to encapsulate all they want to say in one or two brief sentences. For job seekers who are unfocused or unclear about their intentions, trying to write this section can inhibit the entire résumé writing process.

Keep the objective as short as possible and no longer than two short sentences.

Exhibit 2.1
CHRONOLOGICAL RÉSUMÉ

REBEKAH DONAHUE
3530 Buckhorn St.
Jefferson Valley, NY 10534
(914) 555-3434
r.donahue@xxx.com

OBJECTIVE
Motivated, organized, and detail-oriented individual seeking an entry-level position in newspaper editing.

EDUCATION
Fordham University—Bronx, NY
B.A. Communication and Media Studies, concentration in Journalism, May 2006
Major GPA: 4.0

RELEVANT COURSES
- Basic Feature Writing
- Graphics for Publication
- Newsmaking: Interpreting and Reconstructing Reality
- The Journalist and the Law
- Versions of Censorship and Freedom of Expression
- Topics in Writing and Journalism
- Inside the *New York Times*

EXPERIENCE
Intern, New York Times. New York, NY, May 2005–present
Responsibilities include assisting with layout, proofreading, and assisting book
    review editor.
Editorial Assistant, Bronx Times Reporter. Bronx, NY, June 2002–August 2004
Responsibilities included proofreading and providing administrative assistance to
    senior editor.
Administrative Assistant, Journalism Department, Fordham University. Bronx, NY,
    September 2004–May 2005
Provided administrative assistance to faculty members.

continued

SKILLS
Excellent computer and office skills, desktop publishing, fluent in Spanish and
Italian.

REFERENCES
Available upon request.

Choose one of the following types of objective statement:

1. *General Objective Statement*

- An entry-level educational programming coordinator position

2. *Position-Focused Objective*

- To obtain the position of conference coordinator at State College

3. *Industry-Focused Objective*

- To begin a career as a sales representative in the cruise line industry

4. *Summary of Qualifications Statement*

A degree in communications with a concentration in journalism,
combined with a journalism internship and work experience at
a local newspaper, has prepared me for a position in the editorial department of a newspaper that values determination and
attention to detail.

Support Your Objective. A résumé that contains any one of these types of
objective statements should then go on to demonstrate why you are qualified
to get the position. Listing academic degrees can be one way to indicate

qualifications. Another demonstration would be in the way previous experiences, both volunteer and paid, are described. Without this kind of documentation in the body of the résumé, the objective looks unsupported. Think of the résumé as telling a connected story about you. All the elements should work together to form a coherent picture that ideally should relate to your statement of objective.

Education

This section of your résumé should indicate the exact name of the degree you will receive or have received, spelled out completely with no abbreviations. The degree is generally listed after the objective, followed by the institution name and location, and then the month and year of graduation. This section could also include your academic minor, grade point average (GPA), and appearance on the Dean's List or President's List.

If you have enough space, you might want to include a section listing courses related to the field in which you are seeking work. The best use of a "related courses" section would be to list some course work that is not traditionally associated with the major. Perhaps you took several computer courses outside your degree that will be helpful and related to the job prospects you are entertaining. Several education section examples are shown here:

- Bachelor of Arts Degree in English; University of Wisconsin, May 2006
- Bachelor of Arts Degree in Communications; Dartmouth College, January 2007; Minor: Technical Writing
- Bachelor of Arts Degree in French; McGill University, May 2006; Minor: Education

An example of a format for a related courses section follows:

RELATED COURSES

Educational Psychology	Research Methods
Journalism Law	Ethics
Creative Writing	

Experience

The experience section of your résumé should be the most substantial part and should take up most of the space on the page. Employers want to see what kind of work history you have. They will look at your range of experiences, longevity in jobs, and specific tasks you are able to complete. This section may also be called "work experience," "related experience," "employment history," or "employment." No matter what you call this section, some important points to remember are the following:

1. **Describe your duties** as they relate to the position you are seeking.
2. **Emphasize major responsibilities** and indicate increases in responsibility. Include all relevant employment experiences: summer, part-time, internships, cooperative education, or self-employment.
3. **Emphasize skills**, especially those that transfer from one situation to another. The fact that you coordinated a student organization, chaired meetings, supervised others, and managed a budget leads one to suspect that you could coordinate other things as well.
4. **Use descriptive job titles** that provide information about what you did. A "Student Intern" should be more specifically stated as, for example, "Magazine Operations Intern." "Volunteer" is also too general; a title such as "Peer Writing Tutor" would be more appropriate.
5. **Create word pictures** by using active verbs to start sentences. Describe *results* you have produced in the work you have done.

A limp description would say something such as the following: "My duties included helping with production, proofreading, and editing. I used a design and page layout program." An action statement would be stated as follows: "Coordinated and assisted in the creative marketing of brochures and seminar promotions, becoming proficient in Quark."

Remember, an accomplishment is simply a result, a final measurable product that people can relate to. A duty is not a result; it is an obligation—every job holder has duties. For an effective résumé, list as many results as you can. To make the most of the limited space you have and to give your description impact, carefully select appropriate and accurate descriptors.

Here are some traits that employers tell us they like to see:

- Teamwork
- Energy and motivation

- Learning and using new skills
- Versatility
- Critical thinking
- Understanding how profits are created
- Organizational acumen
- Communicating directly and clearly, in both writing and speaking
- Risk taking
- Willingness to admit mistakes
- High personal standards

Solutions to Frequently Encountered Problems

Repetitive Employment with the Same Employer

EMPLOYMENT: The Foot Locker, Portland, Oregon. Summer 2001, 2002, 2003. Initially employed in high school as salesclerk. Because of successful performance, asked to return next two summers at higher pay with added responsibility. Ranked as the #2 salesperson the first summer and #1 the next two summers. Assisted in arranging eye-catching retail displays; served as manager of other summer workers during owner's absence.

A Large Number of Jobs

EMPLOYMENT: Recent Hospitality Industry Experience: Affiliated with four upscale hotel/restaurant complexes (September 2001–February 2004), where I worked part- and full-time as a waiter, bartender, disc jockey, and bookkeeper to produce income for college.

Several Positions with the Same Employer

EMPLOYMENT: Coca-Cola Bottling Co., Burlington, Vermont, 2001–2004. In four years, I received three promotions, each with increased pay and responsibility.

Summer Sales Coordinator: Promoted to hire, train, and direct efforts of add-on staff of fifteen college-age route salespeople hired to meet summer peak demand for product.

Sales Administrator: Promoted to run home office sales desk, managing accounts and associated delivery schedules for professional sales force of ten people. Intensive phone work, daily interaction with all personnel, and strong knowledge of product line required.

Route Salesperson: Summer employment to travel and tourism industry sites that use Coke products. Met specific schedule demands, used good communication skills with wide variety of customers, and demonstrated strong selling skills. Named salesperson of the month for July and August of that year.

Questions Résumé Writers Often Ask

How Far Back Should I Go in Terms of Listing Past Jobs?

Usually, listing three or four jobs should suffice. If you did something back in high school that has a bearing on your future aspirations for employment, by all means list the job. As you progress through your college career, high school jobs will be replaced on the résumé by college employment.

Should I Differentiate Between Paid and Nonpaid Employment?

Most employers are not initially concerned about how much you were paid. They are eager to know how much responsibility you held in your past employment. There is no need to specify that your work was as a volunteer if you had significant responsibilities.

How Should I Represent My Accomplishments or Work-Related Responsibilities?

Succinctly, but fully. In other words, give the employer enough information to arouse curiosity but not so much detail that you leave nothing to the imagination. Besides, some jobs merit more lengthy explanations than others. Be sure to convey any information that can give an employer a better understanding of the depth of your involvement at work. Did you supervise others? How many? Did your efforts result in a more efficient operation? How much did you increase efficiency? Did you handle a budget? How much? Were you promoted in a short time? Did you work two jobs at once or fifteen hours per week after high school? Where appropriate, quantify.

Should the Work Section Always Follow the Education Section on the Résumé?

Always lead with your strengths. If your education closely relates to the employment you now seek, put this section after the objective. If your education does not closely relate but you have a surplus of good work experiences, consider reversing the order of your sections to lead with employment, followed by education.

How Should I Present My Activities, Honors, Awards, Professional Societies, and Affiliations?

This section of the résumé can add valuable information for an employer to consider if used correctly. The rule of thumb for information in this section is to include only those activities that are in some way relevant to the objective stated on your résumé. If you can draw a valid connection between your activities and your objective, include them; if not, leave them out.

Professional affiliations and honors should all be listed; especially important are those related to your job objective. Social clubs and activities need not be a part of your résumé unless you hold a significant office or you are looking for a position related to your membership. Be aware that most prospective employers' principal concerns are related to your employability, not your social life. If you have any, publications can be included as an addendum to your résumé.

How Should I Handle References?

The use of references is considered a part of the interview process, and they should never be listed on a résumé. You would always provide references to a potential employer if requested to, so it is not even necessary to include this section on the résumé if space does not permit. If space is available, it is acceptable to include the following statement:

- References furnished upon request.

The Functional Résumé

The functional résumé departs from a chronological résumé in that it organizes information by specific accomplishments in various settings: previous jobs, volunteer work, associations, and so forth. This type of résumé permits you to stress the substance of your experiences rather than the position titles you have held. You should consider using a functional résumé if you have held a series of similar jobs that relied on the same skills or abilities. There are many good books in which you can find examples of functional résumés, including *How to Write a Winning Resume* or *Resumes Made Easy*.

The Targeted Résumé

The targeted résumé focuses on specific work-related capabilities you can bring to a given position within an organization. Past achievements are listed to highlight your capabilities and the work history section is abbreviated.

Digital Résumés

Today's employers have to manage an enormous number of résumés. One of the most frequent complaints the writers of this series hear from students is the failure of employers to even acknowledge the receipt of a résumé and cover letter. Frequently, the reason for this poor response or nonresponse is the volume of applications received for every job. In an attempt to better manage the considerable labor investment involved in processing large numbers of résumés, many employers are requiring digital submission of résumés. There are two types of digital résumés: those that can be e-mailed or posted to a website, called *electronic résumés*, and those that can be "read" by a computer, commonly called *scannable résumés*. Though the format may be a bit different from the traditional "paper" résumé, the goal of both types of digital résumés is the same—to get you an interview! These résumés must be designed to be "technologically friendly." What that basically means to you is that they should be free of graphics and fancy formatting. (See Exhibit 2.2.)

Electronic Résumés

Sometimes referred to as plain-text résumés, electronic résumés are designed to be e-mailed to an employer or posted to one of many commercial Internet databases such as Careerbuilder.com, America's Job Bank (ajb.dni.us), or Monster.com.

Some technical considerations:

- Electronic résumés must be written in American Standard Code for Information Interchange (ASCII), which is simply a plain-text format. These characters are universally recognized so that every computer can accurately read and understand them. To create an ASCII file of your current résumé, open your document, then save it as a text or ASCII file. This will eliminate all formatting. Edit as needed using your computer's text editor application.
- Use a standard-width typeface. Courier is a good choice because it is the font associated with ASCII in most systems.

Exhibit 2.2
DIGITAL RÉSUMÉ

REBEKAH DONAHUE
3530 Buckhorn St.
Jefferson Valley, NY 10534
(914) 555-3434
r.donahue@xxx.com

Put your name at the top on its own line.

Put your phone number on its own line.

KEYWORD SUMMARY
Desktop publishing
Ethical journalism
Feature writing
Graphics

Keywords make your résumé easier to find in a database.

EDUCATION
Fordham University—Bronx, NY
B.A. Communication and Media Studies
Concentration in Journalism, May 2006
Major GPA: 4.0

Use a standard-width typeface.

RELEVANT COURSES
* Basic Feature Writing
* Graphics for Publication
* Newsmaking: Interpreting and Reconstructing Reality
* The Journalist and the Law
* Versions of Censorship and Freedom of Expression
* Topics in Writing and Journalism
* Inside the *New York Times*

No line should exceed sixty-five characters.

Capitalize letters to emphasize headings.

EXPERIENCE
Fordham University, Journalism Department
Administrative Assistant, September 2004-May 2005
Provided administrative assistance to faculty members.
Bronx Times Reporter

End each line by hitting the ENTER (or RETURN) key.

Editorial Assistant, June 2002-August 2004
Responsibilities included proofreading, assisting with layout,
    providing administrative assistance to senior editor.
New York Times
Internship, May 2005-present
Responsibilities include assisting with layout and graphic design.

- Use a font size of 11 to 14 points. A 12-point font is considered standard.
- Your margin should be left-justified.
- Do not exceed sixty-five characters per line because the word-wrap function doesn't operate in ASCII.
- Do not use boldface, italics, underlining, bullets, or various font sizes. Instead, use asterisks, plus signs, or all capital letters when you want to emphasize something.
- Avoid graphics and shading.
- Use as many "keywords" as you possibly can. These are words or phrases usually relating to skills or experience that either are specifically used in the job announcement or are popular buzzwords in the industry.
- Minimize abbreviations.
- Your name should be the first line of text.
- Conduct a "test run" by e-mailing your résumé to yourself and a friend before you send it to the employer. See how it transmits, and make any changes you need to. Continue to test it until it's exactly how you want it to look.
- Unless an employer specifically requests that you send the résumé in the form of an attachment, don't. Employers can encounter problems opening a document as an attachment, and there are always viruses to consider.
- Don't forget your cover letter. Send it along with your résumé as a single message.

Scannable Résumés

Some companies are relying on technology to narrow the candidate pool for available job openings. Electronic Applicant Tracking uses imaging to scan, sort, and store résumé elements in a database. Then, through OCR (Optical Character Recognition) software, the computer scans the résumés for keywords and phrases. To have the best chance at getting an interview, you want to increase the number of "hits"—matches of your skills, abilities, experience, and education to those the computer is scanning for—your résumé will get. You can see how critical using the right keywords is for this type of résumé.

Technical considerations include:

- Again, do not use boldface (newer systems may be able to read this, but many older ones won't), italics, underlining, bullets, shading, graphics, or multiple font sizes. Instead, for emphasis, use asterisks, plus signs, or all capital letters. Minimize abbreviations.

- Use a popular typeface such as Courier, Helvetica, Arial, or Palatino. Avoid decorative fonts.
- Font size should be between 11 and 14 points.
- Do not compress the spacing between letters.
- Use horizontal and vertical lines sparingly; the computer may misread them as the letters *L* or *I*.
- Left-justify the text.
- Do not use parentheses or brackets around telephone numbers, and be sure your phone number is on its own line of text.
- Your name should be the first line of text and on its own line. If your résumé is longer than one page, be sure to put your name on the top of all pages.
- Use a traditional résumé structure. The chronological format may work best.
- Use nouns that are skill-focused, such as *management, writer,* and *programming.* This is different from traditional paper résumés, which use action-oriented verbs.
- Laser printers produce the finest copies. Avoid dot-matrix printers.
- Use standard, light-colored paper with text on one side only. Since the higher the contrast, the better, your best choice is black ink on white paper.
- Always send original copies. If you must fax, set the fax on fine mode, not standard.
- Do not staple or fold your résumé. This can confuse the computer.
- Before you send your scannable résumé, be certain the employer uses this technology. If you can't determine this, you may want to send two versions (scannable and traditional) to be sure your résumé gets considered.

Résumé Production and Other Tips

An ink-jet printer is the preferred option for printing your résumé. Begin by printing just a few copies. You may find a small error or you may simply want to make some changes, and it is less frustrating and less expensive if you print in small batches.

Résumé paper color should be carefully chosen. You should consider the types of employers who will receive your résumé and the types of positions for which you are applying. Use white or ivory paper for traditional or conservative employers or for higher-level positions.

Black ink on sharp, white paper can be harsh on the reader's eyes. Think about an ivory or cream paper that will provide less contrast and be easier to read. Pink, green, and blue tints should generally be avoided.

Many résumé writers buy packages of matching envelopes and cover sheet stationery that, although not absolutely necessary, help convey a professional impression.

If you'll be producing many cover letters at home, be sure you have high-quality printing equipment. Learn standard envelope formats for business, and retain a copy of every cover letter you send out. You can use the copies to take notes of any telephone conversations that may occur.

If attending a job fair, either carry a briefcase or place your résumé in a nicely covered legal-size pad holder.

The Cover Letter

The cover letter provides you with the opportunity to tailor your résumé by telling the prospective employer how you can be a benefit to the organization. It allows you to highlight aspects of your background that are not already discussed in your résumé and that might be especially relevant to the organization you are contacting or to the position you are seeking. Every résumé should have a cover letter enclosed when you send it out. Unlike the résumé, which may be mass-produced, a cover letter is most effective when it is individually prepared and focused on the particular requirements of the organization in question.

A good cover letter should supplement the résumé and motivate the reader to review the résumé. The format shown in Exhibit 2.3 (see page 32) is only a suggestion to help you decide what information to include in a cover letter.

Begin the cover letter with your street address six lines down from the top. Leave three to five lines between the date and the name of the person to whom you are addressing the cover letter. Make sure you leave one blank line between the salutation and the body of the letter and between paragraphs. After typing "Sincerely," leave four blank lines and type your name. This should leave plenty of room for your signature. A sample cover letter is shown in Exhibit 2.4 on page 33.

The following guidelines will help you write good cover letters:

1. Be sure to type your letter neatly; ensure there are no misspellings.
2. Avoid unusual typefaces, such as script.

3. Address the letter to an individual, using the person's name and title. To obtain this information, call the company. If answering a blind newspaper advertisement, address the letter "To Whom It May Concern" or omit the salutation.
4. Be sure your cover letter directly indicates the position you are applying for and tells why you are qualified to fill it.
5. Send the original letter, not a photocopy, with your résumé. Keep a copy for your records.
6. Make your cover letter no more than one page.
7. Include a phone number where you can be reached.
8. Avoid trite language and have someone read the letter over to react to its tone, content, and mechanics.
9. For your own information, record the date you send out each letter and résumé.

Exhibit 2.3
COVER LETTER FORMAT

Your Street Address
Your Town, State, Zip
Phone Number
Fax Number
Date   E-mail

Name
Title
Organization
Address

Dear _____:

First Paragraph. In this paragraph state the reason for the letter, name the specific position or type of work you are applying for, and indicate from which resource (career services office, website, newspaper, contact, employment service) you learned of this opening. The first paragraph can also be used to inquire about future openings.

Second Paragraph. Indicate why you are interested in this position, the company, or its products or services and what you can do for the employer. If you are a recent graduate, explain how your academic background makes you a qualified candidate. Try not to repeat the same information found in the résumé.

Third Paragraph. Refer the reader to the enclosed résumé for more detailed information.

Fourth Paragraph. In this paragraph say what you will do to follow up on your letter. For example, state that you will call by a certain date to set up an interview or to find out if the company will be recruiting in your area. Finish by indicating your willingness to answer any questions the recipient may have. Be sure you have provided your phone number.

Sincerely,

Type your name

Enclosure

Exhibit 2.4
SAMPLE COVER LETTER

72 Ocean Road
Narragansett, RI 02882
(401) 555-8976

May 2, 2007

Raymond Porter
Director
Worcester Community Services
143 Park Lane
Worcester, MA 01653

Dear Mr. Porter:

I am about to graduate from the University of Rhode Island College of Human Science and Services with a master of arts degree in counseling, with a concentration in gerontological counseling. I have read your advertisement for a gerontological counselor and believe that I have the qualifications you are looking for.

The experience that I gained volunteering at South Bay Manor in Kingston, Rhode Island, a combined assisted living and skilled nursing facility, has given me the opportunity to work with geriatric patients at all levels of mobility and health. I have also spent an internship at the Warwick Neck Alzheimer's Center, where I interacted with patients suffering from varying degrees of Alzheimer's disease, as well as their families. Both of these positions helped me gain a firsthand understanding of the needs of geriatric patients and their caregivers, as well as to sharpen my skills in communication, creative thinking, and facilitating discussion.

In addition to the program in gerontology, I also took courses in physical therapy, communicative disorders, and information technology, which I feel give me a more well-rounded foundation for a career in counseling. I believe that my experience combined with my enthusiasm for working with the elderly make me an ideal candidate for the counseling position that you have available.

continued

I would appreciate the opportunity to meet with you to discuss how my education and experience may benefit your organization. I will contact your office early next week to discuss the possibility of an interview. I have enclosed my résumé for your review, and if you have any questions or require any additional information, please contact me at my home, (401) 555-8976.

Sincerely,

Carla Morales

Enclosure

3

Researching Careers and Networking

What do they call the job you want? One reason for confusion is perhaps a mistaken assumption that a college education provides job training. In most cases it does not. Of course, applied fields such as engineering, management, or education provide specific skills for the workplace as well as an education. Regardless, your overall college education exposes you to numerous fields of study and teaches you quantitative reasoning, critical thinking, writing, and speaking, all of which can be successfully applied to a number of different job fields. But it still remains up to you to choose a job field and to learn how to articulate the benefits of your education in a way the employer will appreciate.

"What can I do with my degree?" is a question heard frequently by career counselors. Many liberal arts majors ask this question because, unlike their peers in more specifically focused disciplines such as accounting or information science, they often feel confused about what options are available to them. Without the defined path followed by so many other students, liberal arts majors wonder just what types of careers they can pursue.

Collect Job Titles

The world of employment is a complex place, so you need to become a bit of an explorer and adventurer and be willing to try a variety of techniques to develop a list of possible occupations that might use your talents and education. You might find computerized interest inventories, reference books and other sources, and classified ads helpful in this respect. Once you have a list of possibilities that you are interested in and qualified for, you can move on to find out what kinds of organizations have these job titles.

Computerized Interest Inventories

One way to begin collecting job titles is to identify a number of jobs that call for your degree and the particular skills and interests you identified as part of the self-assessment process. There are excellent interactive career-guidance programs on the market to help you produce such selected lists of possible job titles. Most of these are available at colleges and at some larger town and city libraries. Two of the industry leaders are CHOICES and DISCOVER. Both allow you to enter interests, values, educational background, and other information to produce lists of possible occupations and industries. Each of the resources listed here will produce different job title lists. Some job titles will appear again and again, while others will be unique to a particular source. Investigate all of them!

Reference Sources

Books on the market that may be available through your local library or career counseling office also suggest various occupations related to specific majors. The following are only a few of the many good books on the market: *The College Board Guide to 150 Popular College Majors* and *College Majors and Careers: A Resource Guide for Effective Life Planning* both by Paul Phifer, and *Kaplan's What to Study: 101 Fields in a Flash*. All of these books list possible job titles within the academic major.

Not every employer looking to hire a liberal arts major may be equally appealing to you; some situations may be more attractive than others. For example, a counselor who wants to work with substance-abuse patients could do so working for a government agency, a hospital, or another nonprofit organization. Each environment presents a different "culture," with associated expectations in terms of work, the subject matter of interest, and the outlooks and background of its employees. Although the job titles may be the same, not all locations present the same "fit" for you.

If you majored in another area of liberal arts, such as a foreign language, and have also developed strong writing and research skills, you might be thinking of a career teaching college students. But a language major with these skills might also go on to work in foreign service, in publishing, or for other employers in international settings. Remember that you might find the opportunity to do work you enjoy in a number of varied settings.

Each job title deserves your consideration. Like removing the layers of an onion, the search for job titles can go on and on! As you spend time doing this activity, you are actually learning more about the value of your degree. What's important in your search at this point is not to become critical or selective but rather to develop as long a list of possibilities as you can. Every source used will help you add new and potentially exciting jobs to your growing list.

Classified Ads

It has been well publicized that the classified ad section of the newspaper represents only a small fraction of the current job market. Nevertheless, the weekly classified ads can be a great help to you in your search. Although they may not be the best place to look for a job, they can teach you a lot about the job market. Classified ads provide a good education in job descriptions, duties, responsibilities, and qualifications. In addition, they provide insight into which industries are actively recruiting and some indication of the area's employment market. This is particularly helpful when seeking a position in a specific geographic area and/or a specific field. For your purposes, classified ads are a good source for job titles to add to your list.

Read the Sunday classified ads in a major market newspaper for several weeks in a row. Cut and paste all the ads that interest you and seem to call for something close to your education, skills, experience, and interests. Remember that classified ads are written for what an organization *hopes* to find; you don't have to meet absolutely every criterion. However, if certain requirements are stated as absolute minimums and you cannot meet them, it's best not to waste your time and that of the employer.

The weekly classified want ads exercise is important because these jobs are out in the marketplace. They truly exist, and people with your qualifications are being sought to apply. What's more, many of these advertisements describe the duties and responsibilities of the job advertised and give you a beginning sense of the challenges and opportunities such a position presents. Some will indicate salary, and that will be helpful as well. This information will better define the jobs for you and provide some good material for possible interviews in that field.

Explore Job Descriptions

Once you've arrived at a solid list of possible job titles that interest you and for which you believe you are somewhat qualified, it's a good idea to do some research on each of these jobs. The preeminent source for such job information is the *Dictionary of Occupational Titles*, or *DOT* (wave.net/upg/ immigration/dot_index.html). This directory lists every conceivable job and provides excellent up-to-date information on duties and responsibilities, interactions with associates, and day-to-day assignments and tasks. These descriptions provide a thorough job analysis, but they do not consider the possible employers or the environments in which a job may be performed. So, although a position as public relations officer may be well defined in terms of duties and responsibilities, it does not explain the differences in doing public relations work in a college or a hospital or a factory or a bank. You will need to look somewhere else for work settings.

Learn More About Possible Work Settings

After reading some job descriptions, you may choose to edit and revise your list of job titles once again, discarding those you feel are not suitable and keeping those that continue to hold your interest. Or you may wish to keep your list intact and see where these jobs may be located. For example, if you are interested in public relations and you appear to have those skills and the requisite education, you'll want to know which organizations do public relations. How can you find that out? How much income does someone in public relations make a year and what is the employment potential for the field of public relations?

To answer these and many other questions about your list of job titles, we recommend you try any of the following resources: *Careers Encyclopedia*, the professional societies and resources found throughout this book, *College to Career: The Guide to Job Opportunities*, and the *Occupational Outlook Handbook* (http://stats.bls.gov/ocohome.htm). Each of these resources, in a different way, will help to put the job titles you have selected into an employer context. Perhaps the most extensive discussion is found in the *Occupational Outlook Handbook*, which gives a thorough presentation of the nature of the work, the working conditions, employment statistics, training, other qualifications, and advancement possibilities as well as job outlook and earnings. Related occupations are also detailed, and a select bibliography is provided to help you find additional information.

Continuing with our public relations example, your search through these reference materials would teach you that the public relations jobs you find attractive are available in larger hospitals, financial institutions, most corporations (both consumer goods and industrial goods), media organizations, and colleges and universities.

Networking

Networking is the process of deliberately establishing relationships to get career-related information or to alert potential employers that you are available for work. Networking is critically important to today's job seeker for two reasons: it will help you get the information you need, and it can help you find out about *all* of the available jobs.

Get the Information You Need

Networkers will review your résumé and give you feedback on its effectiveness. They will talk about the job you are looking for and give you a candid appraisal of how they see your strengths and weaknesses. If they have a good sense of the industry or the employment sector for that job, you'll get their feelings on future trends in the industry as well. Some networkers will be very forthcoming about salaries, job-hunting techniques, and suggestions for your job search strategy. Many have been known to place calls right from the interview desk to friends and associates who might be interested in you. Each networker will make his or her own contribution, and each will be valuable.

Because organizations must evolve to adapt to current global market needs, the information provided by decision makers within various organizations will be critical to your success as a new job market entrant. For example, you might learn about the concept of virtual organizations from a networker. Virtual organizations coordinate economic activity to deliver value to customers by using resources outside the traditional boundaries of the organization. This concept is being discussed and implemented by chief executive officers of many organizations, including Ford Motor, Dell, and IBM. Networking can help you find out about this and other trends currently affecting the industries under your consideration.

Find Out About All of the Available Jobs

Not every job that is available at this very moment is advertised for potential applicants to see. This is called the *hidden job market*. Only 15 to 20 percent of all jobs are formally advertised, which means that 80 to 85 percent of available jobs do not appear in published channels. Networking will help you become more knowledgeable about all the employment opportunities available during your job search period.

Although someone you might talk to today doesn't know of any openings within his or her organization, tomorrow or next week or next month an opening may occur. If you've taken the time to show an interest in and knowledge of their organization, if you've shown the company representative how you can help achieve organizational goals and that you can fit into the organization, you'll be one of the first candidates considered for the position.

Networking: A Proactive Approach

Networking is a proactive rather than a reactive approach. You, as a job seeker, are expected to initiate a certain level of activity on your own behalf; you cannot afford to simply respond to jobs listed in the newspaper. Being proactive means building a network of contacts that includes informed and interested decision makers who will provide you with up-to-date knowledge of the current job market and increase your chances of finding out about employment opportunities appropriate for your interests, experience, and level of education. An old axiom of networking says, "You are only two phone calls away from the information you need." In other words, by talking to enough people, you will quickly come across someone who can offer you help.

Preparing to Network

In deliberately establishing relationships, maximize your efforts by organizing your approach. Five specific areas in which you can organize your efforts include reviewing your self-assessment, reviewing your research on job sites and organizations, deciding who you want to talk to, keeping track of all your efforts, and creating your self-promotion tools.

Review Your Self-Assessment

Your self-assessment is as important a tool in preparing to network as it has been in other aspects of your job search. You have carefully evaluated your personal traits, personal values, economic needs, longer-term goals, skill base, preferred skills, and underdeveloped skills. During the networking process you will be called upon to communicate what you know about yourself and relate it to the information or job you seek. Be sure to review the exercises that you completed in the self-assessment section of this book in preparation for networking. We've explained that you need to assess which skills you have acquired from your major that are of general value to an employer; be ready to express those in ways he or she can appreciate as useful in the organizations.

Review Research on Job Sites and Organizations

In addition, individuals assisting you will expect that you'll have at least some background information on the occupation or industry of interest to you. Refer to the appropriate sections of this book and other relevant publications to acquire the background information necessary for effective networking. They'll explain how to identify not only the job titles that might be of interest to you but also which kinds of organizations employ people to do that job. You will develop some sense of working conditions and expectations about duties and responsibilities—all of which will be of help in your networking interviews.

Decide Who You Want to Talk To

Networking cannot begin until you decide who you want to talk to and, in general, what type of information you hope to gain from your contacts. Once you know this, it's time to begin developing a list of contacts. Five useful sources for locating contacts are described here.

College Alumni Network. Most colleges and universities have created a formal network of alumni and friends of the institution who are particularly interested in helping currently enrolled students and graduates of their alma mater gain employment-related information.

It is usually a simple process to make use of an alumni network. Visit your college's website and locate the alumni office and/or your career center. Either or both sites will have information about your school's alumni network. You'll be provided with information on shadowing experiences, geographic information, or those alumni offering job referrals. If you don't find what you're looking for, don't hesitate to phone or e-mail your career center and ask what they can do to help you connect with an alum.

Alumni networkers may provide some combination of the following services: day-long shadowing experiences, telephone interviews, in-person interviews, information on relocating to given geographic areas, internship information, suggestions on graduate school study, and job vacancy notices.

Present and Former Supervisors. If you believe you are on good terms with present or former job supervisors, they may be an excellent resource for providing information or directing you to appropriate resources that would have information related to your current interests and needs. Additionally, these supervisors probably belong to professional organizations that they might be willing to utilize to get information for you.

Employers in Your Area. Although you may be interested in working in a geographic location different from the one where you currently reside, don't overlook the value of the knowledge and contacts those around you are able to provide. Use the local telephone directory and newspaper to identify the types of organizations you are thinking of working for or professionals who have the kinds of jobs you are interested in. Recently, a call made to a local hospital's financial administrator for information on working in health-care financial administration yielded more pertinent information on training seminars, regional professional organizations, and potential employment sites than a national organization was willing to provide.

Employers in Geographic Areas Where You Hope to Work. If you are thinking about relocating, identifying prospective employers or informational contacts in the new location will be critical to your success. Here are some tips for online searching. First, use a "metasearch" engine to get the most out of your search. Metasearch engines combine several engines into one powerful tool. We frequently use dogpile.com and metasearch.com for this purpose. Try using the city and state as your keywords in a search. *New Haven, Connecticut* will bring you to the city's website with links to the chamber of commerce, member businesses, and other valuable resources. By using looksmart.com you can locate newspapers in any area, and they, too, can provide valuable insight before you relocate. Of course, both dogpile and metasearch can lead you to yellow and white page directories in areas you are considering.

Professional Associations and Organizations. Professional associations and organizations can provide valuable information in several areas: career paths that you might not have considered, qualifications relating to those career choices, publications that list current job openings, and workshops or seminars that will enhance your professional knowledge and skills. They can also be excellent sources for background information on given industries: their health, current problems, and future challenges.

There are several excellent resources available to help you locate professional associations and organizations that would have information to meet your needs. Two especially useful publications are the *Encyclopedia of Associations* and *National Trade and Professional Associations of the United States.*

Keep Track of All Your Efforts

It can be difficult, almost impossible, to remember all the details related to each contact you make during the networking process, so you will want to develop a record-keeping system that works for you. Formalize this process by using your computer to keep a record of the people and organizations you want to contact. You can simply record the contact's name, address, and telephone number, and what information you hope to gain.

You could record this as a simple Word document and you could still use the "Find" function if you were trying to locate some data and could only recall the firm's name or the contact's name. If you're comfortable with database management and you have some database software on your computer, then you can put information at your fingertips even if you have only the zip code! The point here is not technological sophistication but good record keeping.

Once you have created this initial list, it will be helpful to keep more detailed information as you begin to actually make the contacts. Those details should include complete contact information, the date and content of each contact, names and information for additional networkers, and required follow-up. Don't forget to send a letter thanking your contact for his or her time! Your contact will appreciate your recall of details of your meetings and conversations, and the information will help you to focus your networking efforts.

Create Your Self-Promotion Tools

There are two types of promotional tools that are used in the networking process. The first is a résumé and cover letter, and the second is a one-minute "infomercial," which may be given over the telephone or in person.

Techniques for writing an effective résumé and cover letter are discussed in Chapter 2. Once you have reviewed that material and prepared these important documents, you will have created one of your self-promotion tools.

The one-minute infomercial will demand that you begin tying your interests, abilities, and skills to the people or organizations you want to network with. Think about your goal for making the contact to help you understand what you should say about yourself. You should be able to express yourself easily and convincingly. If, for example, you are contacting an alumnus of your institution to obtain the names of possible employment sites in a distant city, be prepared to discuss why you are interested in moving to that location, the types of jobs you are interested in, and the skills and abilities you possess that will make you a qualified candidate.

To create a meaningful one-minute infomercial, write it out, practice it as if it will be a spoken presentation, rewrite it, and practice it again if necessary until expressing yourself comes easily and is convincing.

Here's a simplified example of an infomercial for use over the telephone:

Hello, Mr. Reynolds. My name is Ryan O'Connor. I have recently graduated from the University of British Columbia and hope to enter the field of family counseling. I attended the university's School of Social Work and Family Studies, and I feel confident that I have many of the skills required for counselors, such as observation, writing reports, and the ability to listen. I am also comfortable interacting with people who face a variety of problems.

Mr. Reynolds, I'm calling you because I still need more information about the field of family counseling. I'm hoping that you will have the time to sit down with me for maybe a half hour to discuss your insights into family counseling. I would appreciate your views on the various employment settings that I might investigate.

Will it be possible for you to meet with me? I will be able to schedule a meeting at your convenience.

It very well may happen that your employer contact wishes you to communicate by e-mail. The infomercial quoted above could easily be rewritten for an e-mail message. You should "cut and paste" your résumé right into the e-mail text itself.

Other effective self-promotion tools include portfolios for those in the arts, writing professions, or teaching. Portfolios show examples of work, photographs of projects or classroom activities, or certificates and credentials that are job related. There may not be an opportunity to use the portfolio during an interview, and it is not something that should be left with the organization. It is designed to be explained and displayed by the creator. However, during some networking meetings, there may be an opportunity to illustrate a point or strengthen a qualification by exhibiting the portfolio.

Beginning the Networking Process

Set the Tone for Your Communications

It can be useful to establish "tone words" for any communications you embark upon. Before making your first telephone call or writing your first letter, decide what you want the person to think of you. If you are networking to try to obtain a job, your tone words might include descriptors such as *genuine*, *informed*, and *self-knowledgeable*. When you're trying to acquire information, your tone words may have a slightly different focus, such as *courteous*, *organized*, *focused*, and *well-spoken*. Use the tone words you establish for your contacts to guide you through the networking process.

Honestly Express Your Intentions

When contacting individuals, it is important to be honest about your reasons for making the contact. Establish your purpose in your own mind and be able and ready to articulate it concisely. Determine an initial agenda, whether it be informational questioning or self-promotion, present it to your contact, and be ready to respond immediately. If you don't adequately prepare before initiating your overture, you may find yourself at a disadvantage if you're asked to immediately begin your informational interview or self-promotion during the first phone conversation or visit.

Start Networking Within Your Circle of Confidence

Once you have organized your approach—by utilizing specific researching methods, creating a system for keeping track of the people you will contact, and developing effective self-promotion tools—you are ready to begin networking. The best way to begin networking is by talking with a group of people you trust and feel comfortable with. This group is usually made up of your family, friends, and career counselors. No matter who is in this inner circle, they will have a special interest in seeing you succeed in your job search. In addition, because they will be easy to talk to, you should try taking some risks in terms of practicing your information-seeking approach. Gain confidence in talking about the strengths you bring to an organization and the underdeveloped skills you feel hinder your candidacy. Be sure to review the section on self-assessment for tips on approaching each of these areas. Ask for critical but constructive feedback from the people in your circle of confidence on the letters you write and the one-minute infomercial you have developed. Evaluate whether you want to make the changes they suggest, then practice the changes on others within this circle.

Stretch the Boundaries of Your Networking Circle of Confidence

Once you have refined the promotional tools you will use to accomplish your networking goals, you will want to make additional contacts. Because you will not know most of these people, it will be a less comfortable activity to undertake. The practice that you gained with your inner circle of trusted friends should have prepared you to now move outside of that comfort zone.

It is said that any information a person needs is only two phone calls away, but the information cannot be gained until you (1) make a reasonable guess about who might have the information you need and (2) pick up the telephone to make the call. Using your network list that includes alumni, instructors, supervisors, employers, and associations, you can begin preparing your list of questions that will allow you to get the information you need.

Prepare the Questions You Want to Ask

Networkers can provide you with the insider's perspective on any given field and you can ask them questions that you might not want to ask in an interview. For example, you can ask them to describe the more repetitious or mundane parts of the job or ask them for a realistic idea of salary expectations. Be sure to prepare your questions ahead of time so that you are organized and efficient.

Be Prepared to Answer Some Questions

To communicate effectively, you must anticipate questions that will be asked of you by the networkers you contact. Revisit the self-assessment process you undertook and the research you've done so that you can effortlessly respond to questions about your short- and long-term goals and the kinds of jobs you are most interested in pursuing.

General Networking Tips

Make Every Contact Count. Setting the tone for each interaction is critical. Approaches that will help you communicate in an effective way include politeness, being appreciative of time provided to you, and being prepared and thorough. Remember, *everyone* within an organization has a circle of influence, so be prepared to interact effectively with each person you encounter in the networking process, including secretarial and support staff. Many information or job seekers have thwarted their own efforts by being rude to some individuals they encountered as they networked because they made the incorrect assumption that certain persons were unimportant.

Sometimes your contacts may be surprised at their ability to help you. After meeting and talking with you, they might think they have not offered much in the way of help. A day or two later, however, they may make a contact that would be useful to you and refer you to that person.

With Each Contact, Widen Your Circle of Networkers. Always leave an informational interview with the names of at least two more people who can help you get the information or job that you are seeking. Don't be shy about asking for additional contacts; networking is all about increasing the number of people you can interact with to achieve your goals.

Make Your Own Decisions. As you talk with different people and get answers to the questions you pose, you may hear conflicting information or get conflicting suggestions. Your job is to listen to these "experts" and decide what information and which suggestions will help you achieve *your* goals. Only implement those suggestions that you believe will work for you.

Shutting Down Your Network

As you achieve the goals that motivated your networking activity—getting the information you need or the job you want—the time will come to inactivate all or parts of your network. As you do, be sure to tell your primary supporters about your change in status. Call or write to each one of them and give them as many details about your new status as you feel is necessary to maintain a positive relationship.

Because a network takes on a life of its own, activity undertaken on your behalf will continue even after you cease your efforts. As you get calls or are contacted in some fashion, be sure to inform these networkers about your change in status, and thank them for assistance they have provided.

Information on the latest employment trends indicates that workers will change jobs or careers several times in their lifetime. Networking, then, will be a critical aspect in the span of your professional life. If you carefully and thoughtfully conduct your networking activities during your job search, you will have a solid foundation of experience when you need to network the next time around.

Where Are These Jobs, Anyway?

Having a list of job titles that you've designed around your own career interests and skills is an excellent beginning. It means you've really thought about who you are and what you are presenting to the employment market.

It has caused you to think seriously about the most appealing environments to work in, and you have identified some employer types that represent these environments.

The research and the thinking that you've done thus far will be used again and again. They will be helpful in writing your résumé and cover letters, in talking about yourself on the telephone to prospective employers, and in answering interview questions.

Now is a good time to begin to narrow the field of job titles and employment sites down to some specific employers to initiate the employment contact.

Find Out Which Employers Hire People Like You

This section will provide tips, techniques, and specific resources for developing an actual list of specific employers that can be used to make contacts. It is only an outline that you must be prepared to tailor to your own particular needs and according to what you bring to the job search. Once again, it is important to communicate with others along the way exactly what you're looking for and what your goals are for the research you're doing. Librarians, employers, career counselors, friends, friends of friends, business contacts, and bookstore staff will all have helpful information on geographically specific and new resources to aid you in locating employers who'll hire you.

Identify Information Resources

Your interview wardrobe and your new résumé might have put a dent in your wallet, but the resources you'll need to pursue your job search are available for free. The categories of information detailed here are not hard to find and are yours for the browsing.

Numerous resources described in this section will help you identify actual employers. Use all of them or any others that you identify as available in your geographic area. As you become experienced in this process, you'll quickly figure out which information sources are helpful and which are not. If you live in a rural area, a well-planned day trip to a major city that includes a college career office, a large college or city library, state and federal employment centers, a chamber of commerce office, and a well-stocked bookstore can produce valuable results.

There are many excellent resources available to help you identify actual job sites. They are categorized into employer directories (usually indexed by product lines and geographic location), geographically based directories (designed to highlight particular cities, regions, or states), career-specific directories (e.g., *Sports MarketPlace*, which lists tens of thousands of firms involved with sports), periodicals and newspapers, targeted job posting publications, and videos. This is by no means meant to be a complete treatment of resources but rather a starting point for identifying useful resources.

Working from the more general references to highly specific resources, we provide a basic list to help you begin your search. Many of these you'll find easily available. In some cases reference librarians and others will suggest even better materials for your particular situation. Start to create your own customized bibliography of job search references.

Geographically Based Directories. The Job Bank series published by Bob Adams, Inc. (aip.com) contains detailed entries on each area's major employers, including business activity, address, phone number, and hiring contact name. Many listings specify educational backgrounds being sought in potential employees. Each volume contains a solid discussion of each city's or state's major employment sectors. Organizations are also indexed by industry. Job Bank volumes are available for the following places: Atlanta, Boston, Chicago, Dallas–Ft. Worth, Denver, Detroit, Florida, Houston, Los Angeles, Minneapolis, New York, Ohio, Philadelphia, San Francisco, Seattle, St. Louis, Washington, D.C., and other cities throughout the Northwest.

National Job Bank (careercity.com) lists employers in every state, along with contact names and commonly hired job categories. Included are many small companies often overlooked by other directories. Companies are also indexed by industry. This publication provides information on educational backgrounds sought and lists company benefits.

Periodicals and Newspapers. Several sources are available to help you locate which journals or magazines carry job advertisements in your field. Other resources help you identify opportunities in other parts of the country.

- *Where the Jobs Are: A Comprehensive Directory of 1200 Journals Listing Career Opportunities*
- *Corptech Fast 5000 Company Locator*
- *National Ad Search* (nationaladsearch.com)
- *The Federal Jobs Digest* (jobsfed.com) and *Federal Career Opportunities*
- *World Chamber of Commerce Directory* (chamberofcommerce.org)

This list is certainly not exhaustive; use it to begin your job search work.

Targeted Job Posting Publications. Although the resources that follow are national in scope, they are either targeted to one medium of contact (telephone), focused on specific types of jobs, or less comprehensive than the sources previously listed.

- Careers.org (careers.org/index.html)
- *The Job Hunter* (jobhunter.com)

- *Current Jobs for Graduates* (graduatejobs.com)
- *Environmental Opportunities* (ecojobs.com)
- *Y National Vacancy List* (ymca.net/employment/ymca_recruiting/jobright.htm)
- *ArtSEARCH*
- *Community Jobs*
- *National Association of Colleges and Employers: Job Choices series*
- *National Association of Colleges and Employers* (jobweb.com)

Videos. You may be one of the many job seekers who likes to get information via a medium other than paper. Many career libraries, public libraries, and career centers in libraries carry an assortment of videos that will help you learn new techniques and get information helpful in the job search.

Locate Information Resources

Throughout these introductory chapters, we have continually referred you to various websites for information on everything from job listings to career information. Using the Web gives you a mobility at your computer that you don't enjoy if you rely solely on books or newspapers or printed journals. Moreover, material on the Web, if the site is maintained, can be the most up-to-date information available.

You'll eventually identify the information resources that work best for you, but make certain you've covered the full range of resources before you begin to rely on a smaller list. Here's a short list of informational sites that many job seekers find helpful:

- Public and college libraries
- College career centers
- Bookstores
- The Internet
- Local and state government personnel offices
- Career/job fairs

Each one of these sites offers a collection of resources that will help you get the information you need.

As you meet and talk with service professionals at all these sites, be sure to let them know what you're doing. Inform them of your job search, what you've already accomplished, and what you're looking for. The more people who know you're job seeking, the greater the possibility that someone will have information or know someone who can help you along your way.

4

Interviewing and Job Offer Considerations

Certainly, there can be no one part of the job search process more fraught with anxiety and worry than the interview. Yet seasoned job seekers welcome the interview and will often say, "Just get me an interview and I'm on my way!" They understand that the interview is crucial to the hiring process and equally crucial for them, as job candidates, to have the opportunity of a personal dialogue to add to what the employer may already have learned from the résumé, cover letter, and telephone conversations.

Believe it or not, the interview is to be welcomed, and even enjoyed! It is a perfect opportunity for you, the candidate, to sit down with an employer and express yourself and display who you are and what you want. Of course, it takes thought and planning and a little strategy; after all, it *is* a job interview! But it can be a positive, if not pleasant, experience and one you can look back on and feel confident about your performance and effort.

For many new job seekers, a job, any job, seems a wonderful thing. But seasoned interview veterans know that the job interview is an important step for both sides—the employer and the candidate—to see what each has to offer and whether there is going to be a "fit" of personalities, work styles, and attitudes. And it is this concept of balance in the interview, that both sides have important parts to play, that holds the key to success in mastering this aspect of the job search strategy.

Try to think of the interview as a conversation between two interested and equal partners. You both have important, even vital, information to deliver and to learn. Of course, there's no denying the employer has some leverage, especially in the initial interview for recruitment or any interview scheduled by the candidate and not the recruiter. That should not prevent the interviewee from seeking to play an equal part in what should be a fair exchange of information. Too often the untutored candidate allows the interview to become one-sided. The employer asks all the questions and the candidate simply responds. The ideal would be for two mutually interested parties to sit down and discuss possibilities for each. This is a conversation of significance, and it requires preparation, thought about the tone of the interview, and planning of the nature and details of the information to be exchanged.

Preparing for the Interview

The length of most initial interviews is about thirty minutes. Given the brevity, the information that is exchanged ought to be important. The candidate should be delivering material that the employer cannot discover on the résumé, and in turn, the candidate should be learning things about the employer that he or she could not otherwise find out. After all, if you have only thirty minutes, why waste time on information that is already published? The information exchanged is more than just factual, and both sides will learn much from what they see of each other, as well. How the candidate looks, speaks, and acts are important to the employer. The employer's attention to the interview and awareness of the candidate's résumé, the setting, and the quality of information presented are important to the candidate.

Just as the employer has every right to be disappointed when a prospect is late for the interview, looks unkempt, and seems ill-prepared to answer fairly standard questions, the candidate may be disappointed with an interviewer who isn't ready for the meeting, hasn't learned the basic résumé facts, and is constantly interrupted by telephone calls. In either situation there's good reason to feel let down.

There are many elements to a successful interview, and some of them are not easy to describe or prepare for. Sometimes there is just a chemistry between interviewer and interviewee that brings out the best in both, and a good exchange takes place. But there is much the candidate can do to pave the way for success in terms of his or her résumé, personal appearance, goals, and interview strategy—each of which we will discuss. However, none of this preparation is as important as the time and thought the candidate gives to personal self-assessment.

Self-Assessment
Neither a stunning résumé nor an expensive, well-tailored suit can compensate for candidates who do not know what they want, where they are going, or why they are interviewing with a particular employer. Self-assessment, the

process by which we begin to know and acknowledge our own particular blend of education, experiences, needs, and goals, is not something that can be sorted out the weekend before a major interview. Of all the elements of interview preparation, this one requires the longest lead time and cannot be faked.

Because the time allotted for most interviews is brief, it is all the more important for job candidates to understand and express succinctly why they are there and what they have to offer. This is not a time for undue modesty (or for braggadocio either); it is a time for a compelling, reasoned statement of why you feel that you and this employer might make a good match. It means you have to have thought about your skills, interests, and attributes; related those to your life experiences and your own history of challenges and opportunities; and determined what that indicates about your strengths, preferences, values, and areas needing further development.

If you need some assistance with self-assessment issues, refer to Chapter 1. Included are suggested exercises that can be done as needed, such as making up an experiential diary and extracting obvious strengths and weaknesses from past experiences. These simple assignments will help you look at past activities as collections of tasks with accompanying skills and responsibilities. Don't overlook your high school or college career office. Many offer personal counseling on self-assessment issues and may provide testing instruments such as the *Myers-Briggs Type Indicator (MBTI)*, the *Harrington-O'Shea Career Decision-Making System (CDM)*, the *Strong Interest Inventory (SII)*, or any other of a wide selection of assessment tools that can help you clarify some of these issues prior to the interview stage of your job search.

The Résumé

Résumé preparation has been discussed in detail, and some basic examples were provided. In this section we want to concentrate on how best to use your résumé in the interview. In most cases the employer will have seen the résumé prior to the interview, and, in fact, it may well have been the quality of that résumé that secured the interview opportunity.

An interview is a conversation, however, and not an exercise in reading. So, if the employer hasn't seen your résumé and you have brought it along to the interview, wait until asked or until the end of the interview to offer it. Otherwise, you may find yourself staring at the back of your résumé and simply answering "yes" and "no" to a series of questions drawn from that document.

Sometimes an interviewer is not prepared and does not know or recall the contents of the résumé and may use the résumé to a greater or lesser degree as a "prompt" during the interview. It is for you to judge what that may indicate about the individual performing the interview or the employer. If your interviewer seems surprised by the scheduled meeting, relies on the résumé to an inordinate degree, and seems otherwise unfamiliar with your background, this lack of preparation for the hiring process could well be a symptom of general management disorganization or may simply be the result of poor planning on the part of one individual. It is your responsibility as a potential employee to be aware of these signals and make your decisions accordingly.

It is fine for you to guide the conversation back to a more interpersonal style by saying, "Ms. Perkins, you might be interested in some writing experience I gained during an internship that is not detailed on my résumé." This may give you an opportunity to present more information about your strengths and will return the interview to a more interactive conversation.

By all means, bring at least one copy of your résumé to the interview. Occasionally, at the close of an interview, an interviewer will express an interest in circulating a résumé to several departments, and you could then offer the copy you brought. Sometimes, an interview appointment provides an opportunity to meet others in the organization who may express an interest in you and your background, and it may be helpful to follow up with a copy of your résumé. Our best advice, however, is to keep it out of sight until needed or requested.

Employer Information

Whether your interview is for graduate school admission, an overseas corporate position, or a position with a local company, it is important to know something about the employer or the organization. Keeping in mind that the interview is relatively brief and that you will hopefully have other interviews with other organizations, it is important to keep your research in proportion. If secondary interviews are called for, you will have additional time to do further research. For the first interview, it is helpful to know the organization's mission, goals, size, scope of operations, and so forth. Your research may uncover recent areas of challenge or particular successes that may help to fuel the interview. Use the "What Do They Call the Job You Want?" section of Chapter 3, your library, and your career or guidance office to help you locate this information in the most efficient way possible. Don't be shy in asking advice of these counseling and guidance professionals on how best to spend your preparation time. With some practice, you'll soon learn how much information is enough and which kinds of information are most useful to you.

Interview Content

We've already discussed how it can help to think of the interview as an important conversation—one that, as with any conversation, you want to find pleasant and interesting and to leave you with a good feeling. But because this conversation is especially important, the information that's exchanged is critical to its success. What do you want them to know about you? What do you need to know about them? What interview technique do you need to particularly pay attention to? How do you want to manage the close of the interview? What steps will follow in the hiring process?

Except for the professional interviewer, most of us find interviewing stressful and anxiety-provoking. Developing a strategy before you begin interviewing will help you relieve some stress and anxiety. One particular strategy that has worked for many and may work for you is interviewing by objective. Before you interview, write down three to five goals you would like to achieve for that interview. They may be technique goals: smile a little more, have a firmer handshake, be sure to ask about the next stage in the interview process before leaving. They may be content-oriented goals: find out about the company's current challenges and opportunities; be sure to speak of your recent research, writing experiences, or foreign travel. Whatever your goals, jot down a few of them as goals for each interview.

Most people find that in trying to achieve these few goals, their interviewing technique becomes more organized and focused. After the interview, the most common question friends and family ask is "How did it go?" With this technique, you have an indication of whether you met *your* goals for the meeting, not just some vague idea of how it went. Chances are, if you accomplished what you wanted to, it improved the quality of the entire interview. As you continue to interview, you will want to revise your goals to continue improving your interview skills.

Now, add to the concept of the significant conversation the idea of a beginning, a middle, and a closing and you will have two thoughts that will give your interview a distinctive character. Be sure to make your introduction warm and cordial. Say your full name (and if it's a difficult-to-pronounce name, help the interviewer to pronounce it) and make certain you know your interviewer's name and how to pronounce it. Most interviews begin with some "soft talk" about the weather, chat about the candidate's trip to the interview site, or national events. This is done as a courtesy to relax both you and the interviewer, to get you talking, and to generally try to defuse the atmosphere of excessive tension. Try to be yourself, engage in the conversation, and don't try to second-guess the interviewer. This is simply what it appears to be—casual conversation.

Once you and the interviewer move on to exchange more serious information in the middle part of the interview, the two most important concerns become your ability to handle challenging questions and your success at asking meaningful ones. Interviewer questions will probably fall into one of three categories: personal assessment and career direction, academic assessment, and knowledge of the employer. Here are a few examples of questions in each category:

Personal Assessment and Career Direction
1. What motivates you to put forth your best effort?
2. What do you consider to be your greatest strengths and weaknesses?
3. What qualifications do you have that make you think you will be successful in this career?

Academic Assessment
1. What led you to choose your major?
2. What subjects did you like best and least? Why?
3. How has your college experience prepared you for this career?

Knowledge of the Employer
1. What do you think it takes to be successful in an organization like ours?
2. In what ways do you think you can make a contribution to our organization?
3. Why did you choose to seek a position with this organization?

The interviewer wants a response to each question but is also gauging your enthusiasm, preparedness, and willingness to communicate. In each response you should provide some information about yourself that can be related to the employer's needs. A common mistake is to give too much information. Answer each question completely, but be careful not to run on too long with extensive details or examples.

Questions About Underdeveloped Skills

Most employers interview people who have met some minimum criteria of education and experience. They interview candidates to see who they are, to learn what kind of personality they exhibit, and to get some sense of how they might fit into the existing organization. It may be that you are asked about skills the employer hopes to find and that you have not documented. Maybe it's grant-writing experience, knowledge of the European political system, or a knowledge of the film world.

To questions about skills and experiences you don't have, answer honestly and forthrightly and try to offer some additional information about skills you do have. For example, perhaps the employer is disappointed you have no grant-writing experience. An honest answer may be as follows:

No, unfortunately, I was never in a position to acquire those skills. I do understand something of the complexities of the grant-writing process and feel confident that my attention to detail, careful reading skills, and strong writing would make grants a wonderful challenge in a new job. I think I could get up on the learning curve quickly.

The employer hears an honest admission of lack of experience but is reassured by some specific skill details that do relate to grant writing and a confident manner that suggests enthusiasm and interest in a challenge.

For many students, questions about their possible contribution to an employer's organization can prove challenging. Because your education has probably not included specific training for a job, you need to review your academic record and select capabilities you have developed in your major that an employer can appreciate. For example, perhaps you read well and can analyze and condense what you've read into smaller, more focused pieces. That could be valuable. Or maybe you did some serious research and you know you have valuable investigative skills. Your public speaking might be highly developed and you might use visual aids appropriately and effectively. Or maybe your skill at correspondence, memos, and messages is effective. Whatever it is, you must take it out of the academic context and put it into a new, employer-friendly context so your interviewer can best judge how you could help the organization.

Exhibiting knowledge of the organization will, without a doubt, show the interviewer that you are interested enough in the available position to have done some legwork in preparation for the interview. Remember, it is not necessary to know every detail of the organization's history but rather to have a general knowledge about why it is in business and how the industry is faring.

Sometime during the interview, generally after the midway point, you'll be asked if you have any questions for the interviewer. Your questions will tell the employer much about your attitude and your desire to understand the organization's expectations so you can compare them to your own strengths. The following are just a few questions you might want to ask:

1. What is the communication style of the organization? (meetings, memos, and so forth)
2. What would a typical day in this position be like for me?
3. What have been some of the interesting challenges and opportunities your organization has recently faced?

Most interviews draw to a natural closing point, so be careful not to prolong the discussion. At a signal from the interviewer, wind up your presentation, express your appreciation for the opportunity, and be sure to ask what the next stage in the process will be. When can you expect to hear from them? Will they be conducting second-tier interviews? If you are interested and haven't heard, would they mind a phone call? Be sure to collect a business card with the name and phone number of your interviewer. On your way out, you might have an opportunity to pick up organizational literature you haven't seen before.

With the right preparation—a thorough self-assessment, professional clothing, and employer information—you'll be able to set and achieve the goals you have established for the interview process.

Interview Follow-Up

Quite often there is a considerable time lag between interviewing for a position and being hired or, in the case of the networker, between your phone call or letter to a possible contact and the opportunity of a meeting. This can be frustrating. "Why aren't they contacting me?" "I thought I'd get another interview, but no one has telephoned." "Am I out of the running?" You don't know what is happening.

Consider the Differing Perspectives
Of course, there is another perspective—that of the networker or hiring organization. Organizations are complex, with multiple tasks that need to be accomplished each day. Hiring is a discrete activity that does not occur as frequently as other job assignments. The hiring process might have to take

second place to other, more immediate organizational needs. Although it may be very important to you, and it is certainly ultimately significant to the employer, other issues such as fiscal management, planning and product development, employer vacation periods, or financial constraints may prevent an organization or individual within that organization from acting on your employment or your request for information as quickly as you or they would prefer.

Use Your Communications Skills

Good communication is essential here to resolve any anxieties, and the responsibility is on you, the job or information seeker. Too many job seekers and networkers offer as an excuse that they don't want to "bother" the organization by writing letters or calling. Let us assure you here and now, once and for all, that if you are troubling an organization by over-communicating, someone will indicate that situation to you quite clearly. If not, you can only assume you are a worthwhile prospect and the employer appreciates being reminded of your availability and interest. Let's look at follow-up practices in the job interview process and the networking situation separately.

Following Up on the Employment Interview

A brief thank-you note following an interview is an excellent and polite way to begin a series of follow-up communications with a potential employer with whom you have interviewed and want to remain in touch. It should be just that—a thank-you for a good meeting. If you failed to mention some fact or experience during your interview that you think might add to your candidacy, you may use this note to do that. However, this should be essentially a note whose overall tone is appreciative and, if appropriate, indicative of a continuing interest in pursuing any opportunity that may exist with that organization. It is one of the few pieces of business correspondence that may be handwritten, but always use plain, good-quality, standard-size paper.

If, however, at this point you are no longer interested in the employer, the thank-you note is an appropriate time to indicate that. You are under no obligation to identify any reason for not continuing to pursue employment with that organization, but if you are so inclined to indicate your professional reasons (pursuing other employers more akin to your interests, looking for greater income production than this employer can provide, a different geographic location), you certainly may. It should not be written with an eye to negotiation, for it will not be interpreted as such.

As part of your interview closing, you should have taken the initiative to establish lines of communication for continuing information about your candidacy. If you asked permission to telephone, wait a week following your thank-you note, then telephone your contact simply to inquire how things are progressing on your employment status. The feedback you receive here should be taken at face value. If your interviewer simply has no information, he or she will tell you so and indicate whether you should call again and when. Don't be discouraged if this should continue over some period of time.

If during this time something occurs that you think improves or changes your candidacy (some new qualification or experience you may have had), including any offers from other organizations, by all means telephone or write to inform the employer about this. In the case of an offer from a competing but less desirable or equally desirable organization, telephone your contact, explain what has happened, express your real interest in the organization, and inquire whether some determination on your employment might be made before you must respond to this other offer. An organization that is truly interested in you may be moved to make a decision about your candidacy. Equally possible is the scenario in which they are not yet ready to make a decision and so advise you to take the offer that has been presented. Again, you have no ethical alternative but to deal with the information presented in a straightforward manner.

When accepting other employment, be sure to contact any employers still actively considering you and inform them of your new job. Thank them graciously for their consideration. There are many other job seekers out there just like you who will benefit from having their candidacy improved when others bow out of the race. Who knows, you might at some future time have occasion to interact professionally with one of the organizations with which you sought employment. How embarrassing it would be to have someone remember you as the candidate who failed to notify them that you were taking a job elsewhere!

In all of your follow-up communications, keep good notes of whom you spoke with, when you called, and any instructions that were given about return communications. This will prevent any misunderstandings and provide you with good records of what has transpired.

Job Offer Considerations

For many recent college graduates, the thrill of their first job and, for some, the most substantial regular income they have ever earned seems an excess of good fortune coming at once. To question that first income or to be critical in any way of the conditions of employment at the time of the initial offer seems like looking a gift horse in the mouth. It doesn't seem to occur to many new hires even to attempt to negotiate any aspect of their first job. And, as many employers who deal with entry-level jobs for recent college graduates will readily confirm, the reality is that there simply isn't much movement in salary available to these new college recruits. The entry-level hire generally does not have an employment track record on a professional level to provide any leverage for negotiation. Real negotiations on salary, benefits, retirement provisions, and so forth come to those with significant employment records at higher income levels.

Of course, the job offer is more than just money. It can be composed of geographic assignment, duties and responsibilities, training, benefits, health and medical insurance, educational assistance, car allowance or company vehicle, and a host of other items. All of this is generally detailed in the formal letter that presents the final job offer. In most cases this is a follow-up to a personal phone call from the employer representative who has been principally responsible for your hiring process.

That initial telephone offer is certainly binding as a verbal agreement, but most firms follow up with a detailed letter outlining the most significant parts of your employment contract. You may, of course, choose to respond immediately at the time of the telephone offer (which would be considered a binding oral contract), but you will also be required to formally answer the letter of offer with a letter of acceptance, restating the salient elements of the employer's description of your position, salary, and benefits. This ensures that both parties are clear on the terms and conditions of employment and remuneration and any other outstanding aspects of the job offer.

Is This the Job You Want?
Most new employees will respond affirmatively in writing, glad to be in the position to accept employment. If you've worked hard to get the offer and the job market is tight, other offers may not be in sight, so you will say, "Yes, I accept!" What is important here is that the job offer you accept be one that does fit your particular needs, values, and interests as you've outlined them in your self-assessment process. Moreover, it should be a job that will not only use your skills and education but also challenge you to develop new skills and talents.

Jobs are sometimes accepted too hastily, for the wrong reasons, and without proper scrutiny by the applicant. For example, an individual might readily accept a sales job only to find the continual rejection by potential clients unendurable. An office worker might realize within weeks the constraints of a desk job and yearn for more activity. Employment is an important part of our lives. It is, for most of our adult lives, our most continuous productive activity. We want to make good choices based on the right criteria.

If you have a low tolerance for risk, a job based on commission will certainly be very anxiety-provoking. If being near your family is important, issues of relocation could present a decision crisis for you. If you're an adventurous person, a job with frequent travel would provide needed excitement and be very desirable. The importance of income, the need to continue your education, your personal health situation—all of these have an impact on whether the job you are considering will ultimately meet your needs. Unless you've spent some time understanding and thinking about these issues, it will be difficult to evaluate offers you do receive.

More important, if you make a decision that you cannot tolerate and feel you must leave that job, you will then have both unemployment and self-esteem issues to contend with. These will combine to make the next job search tough going, indeed. So make your acceptance a carefully considered decision.

Negotiate Your Offer

It may be that there is some aspect of your job offer that is not particularly attractive to you. Perhaps there is no relocation allotment to help you move your possessions, and this presents some financial hardship for you. It may be that the health insurance is less than you had hoped. Your initial assignment may be different from what you expected, either in its location or in the duties and responsibilities that comprise it. Or it may simply be that the salary is less than you anticipated. Other considerations may be your official starting date of employment, vacation time, evening hours, dates of training programs or schools, and other concerns.

If you are considering not accepting the job because of some item or items in the job offer "package" that do not meet your needs, you should know that most employers emphatically wish that you would bring that issue to their attention. It may be that the employer can alter it to make the offer more agreeable for you. In some cases it cannot be changed. In any event the employer would generally like to have the opportunity to try to remedy a difficulty rather than risk losing a good potential employee over an issue that might have been resolved. After all, they have spent time and funds in securing your services, and they certainly deserve an opportunity to resolve any possible differences.

Honesty is the best approach in discussing any objections or uneasiness you might have over the employer's offer. Having received your formal offer in writing, contact your employer representative and indicate your particular dissatisfaction in a straightforward manner. For example, you might explain that while you are very interested in being employed by this organization, the salary (or any other benefit) is less than you have determined you require. State the terms you need, and listen to the response. You may be asked to put this in writing, or you may be asked to hold off until the firm can decide on a response. If you are dealing with a senior representative of the organization, one who has been involved in hiring for some time, you may get an immediate response or a solid indication of possible outcomes.

Perhaps the issue is one of relocation. Your initial assignment is in the Midwest, and because you had indicated a strong West Coast preference, you are surprised at the actual assignment. You might simply indicate that while you understand the need for the company to assign you based on its needs, you are disappointed and had hoped to be placed on the West Coast. You could inquire if that were still possible and, if not, would it be reasonable to expect a West Coast relocation in the future.

If your request is presented in a reasonable way, most employers will not see this as jeopardizing your offer. If they can agree to your proposal, they will. If not, they will simply tell you so, and you may choose to continue your candidacy with them or remove yourself from consideration. The choice will be up to you.

Some firms will adjust benefits within their parameters to meet the candidate's need if at all possible. If a candidate requires a relocation cost allowance, he or she may be asked to forgo tuition benefits for the first year to accomplish this adjustment. An increase in life insurance may be adjusted by some other benefit trade-off; perhaps a family dental plan is not needed. In these decisions you are called upon, sometimes under time pressure, to know how you value these issues and how important each is to you.

Many employers find they are more comfortable negotiating for candidates who have unique qualifications or who bring especially needed expertise to the organization. Employers hiring large numbers of entry-level college graduates may be far more reluctant to accommodate any changes in offer conditions. They are well supplied with candidates with similar education and experience so that if rejected by one candidate, they can draw new candidates from an ample labor pool.

Compare Offers

The condition of the economy, the job seeker's academic major and particular geographic job market, and individual needs and demands for certain employment conditions may not provide more than one job offer at a time. Some job seekers may feel that no reasonable offer should go unaccepted for the simple fear there won't be another.

In a tough job market, or if the job you seek is not widely available, or when your job search goes on too long and becomes difficult to sustain financially and emotionally, it may be necessary to accept an inferior offer. The alternative is continued unemployment. Even here, when you feel you don't have a choice, you can at least understand that in accepting this particular offer, there may be limitations and conditions you don't appreciate. At the time of acceptance, there were no other alternatives, but you can begin to use that position to gain the experience and talent to move toward a more attractive position.

Sometimes, however, more than one offer is received, and the candidate has the luxury of choice. If the job seeker knows what he or she wants and has done the necessary self-assessment honestly and thoroughly, it may be clear that one of the offers conforms more closely to those expressed wants and needs.

However, if, as so often happens, the offers are similar in terms of conditions and salary, the question then becomes which organization might provide the necessary climate, opportunities, and advantages for your professional development and growth. This is the time when solid employer research and astute questioning during the interviews really pay off. How much did you learn about the employer through your own research and skillful questioning? When the interviewer asked during the interview "Do you have any questions?" did you ask the kinds of questions that would help resolve a choice between one organization and another? Just as an employer must decide among numerous applicants, so must the applicant learn to assess the potential employer. Both are partners in the job search.

Reneging on an Offer

An especially disturbing occurrence for employers and career counseling professionals is when a job seeker formally (either orally or by written contract) accepts employment with one organization and later reneges on the agreement and goes with another employer.

There are all kinds of rationalizations offered for this unethical behavior. None of them satisfies. The sad irony is that what the job seeker is willing to do to the employer—make a promise and then break it—he or she would be outraged to have done to him- or herself: have the job offer pulled. It is a very bad way to begin a career. It suggests the individual has not taken the time to do the necessary self-assessment and self-awareness exercises to think and judge critically. The new offer taken may, in fact, be no better or worse than the one refused. You should be aware that there have been incidents of legal action following job candidates' reneging on an offer. This adds a very sour note to what should be a harmonious beginning of a lifelong adventure.

PART TWO

THE CAREER PATHS

5

Introduction to Liberal Arts Career Paths

In the introduction to this book we discussed some prejudices against liberal arts degrees, specifically that while they provide a well-rounded education, they offer few solid employment skills. To the contrary, the diversity of a liberal arts degree can lead to more employment options than any other area of professional study.

The abilities to think creatively, to solve problems, and to effectively communicate both verbally and in writing are skills highly sought after by employers in a variety of fields—and they are all skills that you can acquire through a liberal arts education.

The Career Paths

The actual career paths open to liberal arts majors are too numerous to include in one book. For the purposes of this book, six major career paths have been identified and examined:

1. Teaching
2. Corporate communications
3. Media
4. Advertising, marketing, and sales
5. The helping professions
6. Law

Some of these paths offer employment opportunities for graduates in any major, others prefer more specific specialization, and still others require graduate school or other additional training.

Furthermore, other related career paths and job settings within these paths are discussed as follows.

Government

Employment opportunities are almost limitless within the various government agencies and departments. Some are identified in the chapters on the helping professions (e.g., working for social service agencies), law (e.g., working for appellate courts or other government employers), and corporate communications (i.e., government functions similarly to most corporations).

Other settings to consider are government security agencies, such as the Federal Bureau of Investigation (FBI) or Central Intelligence Agency (CIA). Even government at the local city and county levels offer positions to bachelor's- and master's-level liberal arts majors.

Business

The category of business is wide open to liberal arts majors. It is so broad that it has been broken down into the areas of corporate communications (e.g., public relations) and advertising, marketing, and sales. The job settings range from the standard corporation or advertising agency to the foreign service and nonprofit associations.

Additional Paths

Other paths not specifically or extensively approached in this book, but equally deserving of consideration for liberal arts majors, include the following.

Nonprofit Agencies

Nonprofits can be the biggest surprise for liberal arts majors. This is a very broad area requiring much of the same expertise as its for-profit cousins. The nonprofit world needs communication specialists in all areas, including advertising and marketing, public relations and publicity, and administration at all levels.

The Sciences

We often think of the sciences as the opposite of liberal arts, but in fact the two can overlap. Although the liberal arts major can rule out all the high-tech and hard sciences, there are still science-related opportunities for liberal arts majors. For example, some people study chemistry or biology and graduate with a B.A. degree. Others pursue a B.S. degree in the various science and science-related fields.

Social Sciences

This book includes the field of psychology under the helping professions. Two other main areas of the social sciences are also open to liberal arts majors: sociology and anthropology, as well as all their various subspecialties.

Music and Art

Music and art are part of the humanities and thus can overlap with liberal arts. Paths open to liberal arts majors in these two fields include teaching, performing, museum work, studio art, and commercial art, among others.

Languages

For the liberal arts major specializing in one or more languages, opportunities include teaching, translating, government work, educational administration, business, industry, and commerce.

History

The history major has many paths to pursue and job settings to work in, from museums to nonprofits, from government to business.

For further help in defining your career path options, other books in the Great Jobs series will lead you to employment possibilities in a variety of fields. They include the following:

- *Great Jobs for Anthropology Majors*
- *Great Jobs for Art Majors*
- *Great Jobs for Biology Majors*
- *Great Jobs for Business Majors*
- *Great Jobs for Communications Majors*
- *Great Jobs for Economics Majors*
- *Great Jobs for Engineering Majors*
- *Great Jobs for English Majors*
- *Great Jobs for Environmental Studies Majors*
- *Great Jobs for Foreign Language Majors*
- *Great Jobs for History Majors*
- *Great Jobs for Music Majors*
- *Great Jobs for Physical Education Majors*
- *Great Jobs for Political Science Majors*
- *Great Jobs for Psychology Majors*
- *Great Jobs for Sociology Majors*
- *Great Jobs for Theater Majors*

New titles are regularly added to the list.

6

Path 1: Teaching

Because a liberal arts course of studies provides an excellent foundation, many majors use their education to prepare for a teaching career. In every liberal arts subject area, teachers are needed at almost all educational levels. However, while many teaching positions are open to job candidates with bachelor's degrees, more and more require advanced degrees. Either a master's or doctorate degree is preferred for most teaching positions, depending on the institution and education level.

Although a liberal arts major will provide a well-rounded education, you will need additional skills to be successful in this extremely important career. The love of teaching and the ability to instruct and share knowledge are even more vital than your love of a particular subject area. Most teachers will tell you that the process of teaching is a give-and-take. Good teachers learn as much from their students as they impart to them.

Definition of the Career Path

An educator can take a variety of career paths and work with many different age groups in many different settings. In this chapter, we will look at the two most traditional teaching paths: kindergarten through secondary school (K–12) and college and university. Alternative suggestions are given later in this chapter under "Related Occupations."

K–12

Teachers work more interactively with their students today than in the past. Students need to be prepared for the future workforce, so the face of education is changing. Schools strive to teach students to interact with others, adapt to new technology, and think through problems logically. Teachers offer the tools and the setting for their students to develop these skills. To encourage collaboration in solving problems, teachers are increasingly having students work in groups to discuss and solve problems together.

Acting as facilitators or coaches, they start dialogs and use direct, hands-on techniques to help students learn and apply concepts in specific subjects. To help children understand abstract concepts, solve problems, and develop critical thought processes, teachers might use props. For example, they teach number concepts or addition and subtraction by playing board games. Older students respond to more sophisticated materials, so teachers might use scientific apparatus, cameras, or computers.

What children learn and experience during their early years can shape their views of themselves and the world. These experiences can also affect their later successes or failures in school, work, and their personal lives. In light of this, kindergarten and elementary-school teachers play a vital role in the development of children as they introduce students to mathematics, language, science, and social studies. They use games, music, artwork, films, books, computers, and other tools to teach basic skills.

More children attend preschool, and they learn mainly through play and interactive activities. Preschool teachers use children's play to encourage language and vocabulary development (e.g., using storytelling, rhyming games, and acting games), improve social skills (e.g., having the children work together to build a neighborhood in a sandbox), and introduce scientific and mathematical concepts (e.g., showing the children how to balance and count blocks when building a bridge or how to mix colors when painting). Kindergarten teachers also use this less-structured approach, which includes small-group lessons, one-on-one instruction, and learning through creative activities such as art, dance, and music. In kindergarten, however, academics begin to take priority. Building on the lessons taught in preschool, children are taught letter recognition, phonics, numbers, and awareness of nature and science.

In most elementary schools, teachers instruct one class of children in several subjects. In some schools, two or more teachers work together as a team and are jointly responsible for a group of students in at least one subject. In other schools, a teacher may teach one specialized subject—perhaps music, art, reading, science, arithmetic, or physical education—to a number of classes. A small but growing number of teachers instruct multilevel classrooms, with students at several different learning levels.

Building on the subjects that were introduced in elementary school, teachers at the middle- and secondary-school levels help students delve more deeply into various academic areas. The students are exposed to more information about the world. These teachers specialize in a specific subject, such as English, Spanish, mathematics, history, or biology. They may also teach career-oriented subjects. Vocational education teachers—also referred to as career and technical or career-technology teachers—instruct and train students to work in a wide variety of fields, such as health care, business, auto repair, communications, and increasingly, technology. They often teach classes that are in high demand by local employers, who may provide input into the curriculum and offer internships to students. Many vocational teachers actively participate in building and overseeing these partnerships. Career guidance and job placement are additional responsibilities of middle- and secondary-school teachers, as well as tracking students after graduation.

The computer has become an integral tool for teachers. Computer resources such as educational software and the Internet promote interactive learning and help teachers present a vast range of experiences to students. The Internet makes communication possible with other students anywhere in the world, to share experiences and different viewpoints. Students often use the Internet to gather information and to do individual research projects. They use computers in other classroom activities as well, such as solving math problems and learning English as a second language. Teachers use computers to record grades and perform other administrative and clerical duties. They must continually update their skills so that they can instruct and use the latest technology in the classroom.

Teachers often work with students from varied ethnic, cultural, and religious backgrounds. With minority populations growing in many areas, teachers must work effectively with a diverse student population. Some schools offer training to help teachers increase their awareness and understanding of different cultures and encourage them to include multicultural programming in their lesson plans.

Appropriate classroom presentations are designed by teachers according to the student's needs and abilities. Teachers plan, evaluate, and assign lessons; prepare, administer, and grade tests; listen to oral presentations; and maintain classroom discipline. Teachers also do individual work with students. They observe and evaluate a student's performance and potential and increasingly use new assessment methods. For example, teachers may examine a portfolio of a student's artwork or writing to judge the overall progress. The teacher would then identify areas where additional assistance is needed. Teachers also grade papers, prepare report cards, and meet with parents and school staff to discuss a student's academic progress or personal problems.

In addition to conducting classroom activities, teachers supervise study halls and homerooms, help facilitate extracurricular activities, and accompany students on field trips. They must be alert to notice students with physical or mental problems and refer them to the proper authorities. Secondary-school teachers occasionally assist students in choosing courses, colleges, and careers. Teachers at all levels also participate in education conferences and workshops.

In recent years, site-based management has gained popularity. It allows teachers and parents to participate actively in management decisions regarding school operations. In many schools, teachers are increasingly involved in making decisions regarding the budget, personnel, textbooks, curriculum design, and teaching methods.

College and University

The faculty at colleges and universities teach and advise more than twenty million full- and part-time students and conduct a significant part of the research in the United States and Canada. They also keep up with new developments in their fields and may consult with government, business, nonprofit, and community organizations.

Based on their academic subject of field, faculty members are divided into departments or divisions. They usually teach several different but related courses in their subject, such as algebra, calculus, and statistics in mathematics, or drama, poetry, and contemporary novel in literature. They may instruct undergraduates, graduate students, or both. College and university faculty may give lectures to several hundred students in large halls, lead small seminars, or supervise students in laboratories. They prepare lectures, exercises, and laboratory experiments; grade exams and papers; and advise and work with students individually. In universities, they also supervise graduate students' teaching and research. College faculty work with an increasingly varied student population that includes growing shares of part-time, older, and culturally and racially diverse students.

To keep abreast of developments in their field, faculty read current literature, interact with colleagues, and participate in professional conferences. Many also conduct their own research; they may perform experiments; collect and analyze data; and examine original documents, literature, and other source material. They then arrive at conclusions and publish their findings in scholarly journals, books, and electronic media.

Many use computer technology extensively, including the Internet, e-mail, CD-ROMs, and software programs such as statistical packages. Many use computers in the classroom as teaching aids and for posting course content, class notes, schedules, and other information on the Internet. The use of e-mail, chat rooms, and other techniques has greatly improved communications between students and teachers, as well as among students.

Many students wish to access their education from remote sites. So some faculty use the Internet to teach distance-learning courses. These are a popular alternative for nontraditional students such as working adults. While this is more convenient for students, the faculty who teach these courses must be able to adapt existing courses to make them successful online or to design a new course that takes advantage of the format.

Most faculty members serve on academic or administrative committees that deal with the policies of their institution, departmental matters, academic issues, curricula, budgets, equipment purchases, and hiring. Some work with student and community organizations. Department chairpersons are faculty members who usually teach some courses but have heavier administrative responsibilities.

The proportion of time spent on research, teaching, administrative work, and other duties varies depending on the type of institution. Faculty members at universities typically spend a significant part of their time on research; those in four-year colleges, somewhat less; and those in two-year colleges, relatively little. However, the teaching load often is heavier in two-year colleges and somewhat lighter at four-year institutions. Regardless of the type of institution, full professors usually spend a greater portion of their time conducting research than do assistant professors, instructors, and lecturers.

Graduate teaching assistants, who may be referred to as TAs, assist faculty, department chairs, or other professional staff by performing teaching or teaching-related duties. Teaching assistants are students who are working toward earning their own graduate degrees; they have their own school commitments in addition to their work responsibilities. Some have full responsibility for teaching a course, usually an introductory one. They need to prepare lectures and exams and assign final grades to students. Other TAs assist faculty members by grading papers, monitoring exams, holding office hours or help-sessions for students, conducting laboratory sessions, or administering quizzes to the class. To determine exactly what is expected of them, teaching assistants usually first meet with the faculty member they will work for, as each faculty member has his or her own needs. For example, some faculty members prefer assistants to sit in on classes, while others assign them other tasks during class time. Graduate teaching assistants may work one-on-one with a faculty member, or they may be one of several assistants for a large class.

Possible Job Settings

Teachers are found in almost every sector of society. In addition to the traditional school or college environment, the following list provides alternative employment settings for those wanting to teach. Each setting has its own requirements and expectations for its teachers, but they all provide an environment where liberal arts majors dedicated to teaching can practice their art.

- Adult-education centers
- Alternative schools
- Community centers
- Community colleges
- Computer online services
- Day-care centers
- Four-year colleges and universities
- Military bases
- Nursery schools
- Overseas language centers
- Overseas schools
- Overseas universities
- Peace Corps
- Prisons and jails
- Private schools
- Public schools
- Recreational centers
- Rehabilitation centers
- Religious organizations
- Vocational and technical schools

Working Conditions

Although teachers at all levels have the same basic goal of providing the best educational opportunities for their students, working conditions vary depending on the grade level and type of institution at which they teach.

K–12

Teachers experience a great deal of satisfaction when their students develop new skills and gain an appreciation of knowledge and learning. However, they can also experience stress and frustration when dealing with unmotivated or disrespectful students, At times, teachers face unruly behavior and even violence in schools. They may also find themselves with large classes or heavy workloads, or they may have to work in old schools that are run down and lack modern amenities. Accountability standards may also contribute to stress, with teachers expected to produce students who can exhibit satisfactory performance on standardized tests in core subjects. Many teachers, particularly in public schools, are also frustrated by the lack of control they have over what they are required to teach.

Teachers in private schools generally enjoy smaller class sizes. They exercise more control in establishing the curriculum and setting standards for performance and discipline. And because private schools can be selective in their admissions processes, students also tend to be more motivated.

Many teachers work more than forty hours a week, including time spent outside the classroom. Part-time schedules are more common among kindergarten teachers. Although some school districts have gone to all-day kindergartens, most teachers at this level still teach two classes a day. The traditional ten-month school year with a two-month vacation during the summer is the norm for most teachers. During the vacation break, they may teach in summer sessions, take other jobs, travel, or pursue personal interests. Many enroll in college courses or workshops to continue their own education. Teachers in districts with a year-round schedule typically work eight weeks in the summer, take a vacation for one week, and have a five-week midwinter break.

Most U.S. states and Canadian provinces have tenure laws that prevent public school teachers from being fired without just cause and due process. Teachers may obtain tenure after they have satisfactorily completed a probationary period of teaching, normally three years. Tenure does not absolutely guarantee a job, but it does provide some security.

College and University
Most full-time college and university teachers have flexible schedules. They teach an average of twelve to sixteen hours per week and must also attend faculty and committee meetings. Most set regular office hours for student consultations, usually from three to six hours per week. Aside from these commitments, teachers are free to decide when and where they will work, and how much time to devote to course preparation, grading, study, research, graduate student supervision, and other activities.

Teaching night and weekend classes is common, particularly at two-year community colleges or institutions with large enrollments of older students who have full-time jobs or family responsibilities. Most colleges and universities require teachers to work nine months of the year, which allows them time to teach additional courses, conduct research, travel, or pursue nonacademic interests during the summer and school holidays. Colleges and universities usually have funds to support the research or other professional development needs of full-time faculty, including travel to conferences and research sites.

Some teachers, known as adjunct faculty, have primary jobs outside of academia, generally in government, private industry, or nonprofit research, and teach as a side job. While some work full-time, the majority of adjunct faculty are part-time teachers. Many prefer to work part-time hours in addition to their primary jobs; some cannot find full-time teaching jobs because of intense competition for available openings. Some work part-time in more than one institution. Adjunct faculty who do not have a doctoral degree are not qualified for tenure-track positions, because they lack a doctoral degree.

University faculty may experience conflict between their responsibilities to teach students and the pressure to conduct research and publish their findings. This may be a particular problem for young faculty seeking advancement in four-year research universities. Also, recent cutbacks in support workers and the hiring of more adjunct faculty have put a greater administrative burden on full-time faculty. Requirements to teach online classes have also increased faculty workloads. Many find it time-consuming to develop courses to put online, in addition to keeping up with the required technology and answering large amounts of e-mail.

Most TAs have flexible work schedules like college and university faculty, but they also must spend a considerable amount of time on their own academic course work and studies. The number of hours they work varies, depending on their assignments. Work may be stressful, particularly when assistants are given full responsibility for teaching a class; however, these students do have the opportunity to gain valuable teaching experience, which is especially helpful for those who hope to become faculty members at colleges and universities.

FIRSTHAND ACCOUNTS FROM TWO EDUCATORS

Read the following accounts from a high school teacher and college professor to gain a sense of what their work entails.

Carol Behan, High School English Teacher

Carol Behan has been teaching for more than thirty-five years and has spent the past twenty-five at Edmeston Central School in Edmeston, New York. She currently teaches English to ninth- and tenth-graders.

The school is small, with an enrollment of 575 students in grades K–12. The English department has three teachers who each have a lot of input and freedom in developing their programs. Carol's classes have anywhere from twelve to twenty-eight students, and she enjoys watching her students' growth from year to year.

Edmeston Central School operates on a rotating schedule, rather than a traditional Monday-through-Friday schedule. Carol describes this as more like college than high school, with each day different from the next. She teaches one section each in literature, writing, and public speaking. Carol is allowed to decide which textbooks to use and has been able to develop the program as she likes it.

On the negative side, Carol acknowledges that teachers often have to find a way to work around administrators or others with decision-making power who may not be qualified or who are unaware of the students' needs. Although she loves teaching, Carol is also aware of the high potential for burnout for those who put too much of themselves into their job. Even teachers in small schools encounter poor attitudes from students, discipline problems, and violence. Carol recalls a student who brought a shotgun into her school and aimed it at a teacher with whom he had a conflict. Such serious problems can occur in schools in any setting, urban or rural.

"It's sad because I love doing what I'm doing," Carol says. "Teaching is a performance art. I love communicating the literature. I teach a real snazzy Shakespeare unit, for example, and I watch the kids really come alive. That's what I went into teaching for."

Getting Started

Carol has a B.A. in liberal arts with a concentration in English from SUNY–Potsdam and a master's degree in reading from SUNY–Cortland. She chose a reading major in order to have more job options.

Teaching was not Carol's first career choice. Although she had the example of her mother, who was a dedicated and talented teacher, Carol had wanted to work as a research scientist because of her father's death from cancer. She admits that that had been an emotional way of choosing a career. Inspired by several of her high-school teachers, in the end Carol decided to get a teaching degree.

Advice from a Professional

Carol advises potential teachers to love their subject matter and recognize its value in people's lives; this is the best way to be a convincing teacher.

"Teachers are role models, we always will be," Carol says. "But our idealism has to be tempered with reality. Some people come in and they bruise so easily—the kids' attitudes can be very tough. Most of it is just for show, testing us, but we have to remember that we do have a lot of influence on

continued

their lives. I think teaching is more important than it's ever been, even though it's harder now than it's ever been."

Marshall J. Cook, Author and Professor, University of Wisconsin, Madison

Marshall J. Cook is a full professor in the department of communication programs within the division of continuing studies at the University of Wisconsin–Madison. He is also a writer with hundreds of articles to his credit, a couple dozen short stories, and numerous books, including *Writing for the Joy of It*, *Freeing Your Creativity*, *How to Write with the Skill of a Master and the Genius of a Child*, *Slow Down . . . and Get More Done*, *Leads and Conclusions*, and *Hometown Wisconsin*. Before coming to Wisconsin, Marshall Cook was an instructor at Solano Community College in Suisun City, California, for eight years.

Marshall describes his current position as different from that of the traditional campus teacher. The division of continuing studies is a separate division within the university and its primary mission is adult education. Marshall conducts workshops and does some consulting and on-site training of newspaper people and corporate communicators. For example, he runs a media workshop for police officers called "Preparing to Be Interviewed by the Press," one on newsletter preparation, and another on stress management that follows his book *Slow Down . . . and Get More Done*. Marshall says, "Basically, I offer anything we can sell to the public. We're an income-generating unit, unlike campus teaching, and we're responsible for paying our own way."

The work is diverse and offers a rare opportunity to combine writing with another career that complements it. He develops workshops and helps publicize them, in addition to his teaching duties. Each year he teaches between sixty and seventy workshops and also does guest-speaking engagements and helps out at other conferences. While this might sound like quite a heavy workload, Marshall points out that there is no research component to his job. His research is all practical, and his publications are all mass media because that's what he teaches. As he says, "The writing helps me teach and the teaching helps me write."

Getting Started

Marshall has a B.A. in creative writing and an M.A. in communications/print journalism from Stanford University. He attended law school for about four months, but realized that although he enjoyed studying the law, he wasn't interested in the actual day-to-day work. He taught one English class at the

University of Santa Clara in California and was hired full-time when a position became available. Marshall worked in the English department for four years and found himself thoroughly enjoying his job, remembering that his dream had always been to be a teacher and writer.

He began working as a member of the academic staff at the University of Wisconsin as a program coordinator. Marshall acknowledges that he's among the last people who entered the system in this way, moving from the academic staff track to a tenure-track position. He became an assistant professor, which is a professor without tenure, worked the required five to six years and applied for tenure at the associate professor level. Three years later he became a full professor.

Advice from a Professional

Although he was able to move directly into a tenure-track position with a master's degree, Marshall advises that today you need a Ph.D. to achieve the same goal.

"It's a wonderful thing to do if you get the chance to do it," he says. "You not only study and discuss interesting ideas, but also share them and watch them grow as you interact with young minds that aren't nearly as trained as yours, but are flexible and hungry for the knowledge you have."

Training and Qualifications

The following are the training requirements needed to teach at different levels.

K–12

To teach in a public school in any of the fifty states and the District of Columbia you must be certified. Certification is generally for one or several related subjects and is granted by the state board of education or a certification advisory committee. You may be certified to teach the early childhood grades (usually nursery school through third grade), the elementary grades (first through sixth or eighth grade), or a special subject, such as reading or music.

In most states, special education teachers receive a credential to teach kindergarten through twelfth grade. These teachers train in the specialty that they choose, for example, teaching children with learning disabilities or behavioral disorders.

Although requirements for regular certificates vary by state, you will need to get a bachelor's degree and to complete an approved teacher-training program that has a prescribed number of subjects, education credits, and a supervised practice teaching practicum. Traditional education programs for kindergarten and elementary-school teachers include courses designed specifically for those preparing to teach in mathematics, physical science, social science, music, art, and literature, as well as prescribed professional education courses such as philosophy of education, psychology of learning, and teaching methods. If you aspire to teach secondary school, you can either major in the subject you plan to teach while also taking education courses, or major in education and take subject courses. Some states require specific grade point averages for teacher certification.

Many states offer alternative teacher certification programs for those who have college training in the subject they will teach but do not have the necessary education courses required for a regular certificate. Originally, alternative certification programs were designed to address teacher shortages in certain subjects, such as mathematics and science, but have since expanded to attract other people into teaching, including recent college graduates and those who are changing careers.

Almost every state requires applicants for teacher certification to be tested for competency in basic skills such as reading and writing, teaching skills, or subject-matter proficiency. Most also require continuing education for renewal of the teacher's certificate; some require a master's degree. Many states have reciprocity agreements that make it easier for teachers who are certified in one state to become certified in another. Teachers may become board-certified by successfully completing the National Board for Professional Teaching Standards certification process. This certification is voluntary, but may result in a higher salary.

In addition to being knowledgeable in their particular subject areas, teachers must be able to communicate, inspire trust and confidence, motivate students, as well as understand their educational and emotional needs. Teachers also should be organized, dependable, patient, and creative.

In Canada, all beginning teachers in public elementary and secondary schools, except those in certain vocational specialties, must have several years of university education in academic and professional subjects and usually must hold a degree. Depending on provincial requirements, one or two years of professional studies must be included in the teacher training program.

The basic teaching requirement in most provinces is a high school education plus four years of college. Since the provinces establish their own standards, you should check with your provincial board for the current certification requirements.

In addition to specific instruction in methods, measurement, and evaluation, your teacher education program will include introductory courses in the history, psychology, philosophy, and sociology of education. You may also choose optional courses dealing with various specializations. A substantial portion of the program is usually devoted to field experiences and to actual teaching practice in classrooms under the supervision of cooperating teachers.

Your application to a teacher education program will most likely include an interview to determine your personal suitability for teaching. Interviewers look for proficiency in English or French, emotional stability, enthusiasm, and a sincere interest in young people. Experience in community activities that involves working with children is considered an asset. Once accepted into a teacher education program, you will find yourself encouraged to continue evaluating your personal suitability for teaching throughout the program.

Once you have begun your teaching career, you are expected to keep up with continuing professional development. This can involve formal graduate study at a university, as well as short courses, workshops, travel programs, use of resource centers, and similar activities. Professional development programs of this type may be sponsored by school boards, community colleges, teacher centers, teachers' associations, and departments of education.

Teachers enter into contract with the employing school board. In most provinces or territories, this means signing a formal contract; in others, a formal letter of acceptance suffices. Except in the case of teachers in their first year or two of employment with a board, the contract continues indefinitely until terminated by either the teacher or the board. School boards must give a reason for terminating a teacher's contract, except in the case of probationary teachers. The teacher may appeal the dismissal to an impartial board of reference or arbitration tribunal.

Because teaching credentials are not necessarily reciprocal among the provinces, teachers who wish to teach in a new province or territory must apply to the appropriate agency for verification of their standing. The Ministries of Education website, oise.utoronto.ca/canedweb/ministries.html, provides specific information for each jurisdiction. Provisional certification may be granted to an incoming teacher whose credentials don't fully meet those required by the new jurisdiction.

College and University

The requirements for college and university teaching are similar in the United States and Canada. Most faculty are in four academic ranks: professor, associate professor, assistant professor, and instructor. Most faculty members are hired as instructors or assistant professors. Four-year colleges and universities generally hire doctoral-degree holders for full-time, tenure-track positions, but they may hire master's degree holders or doctoral candidates for certain disciplines, such as the arts, or for part-time and temporary jobs. In two-year colleges, master's degree holders often qualify for full-time positions.

Doctoral programs usually take four to seven years of full-time study beyond the bachelor's degree. Candidates usually specialize in a subfield of a discipline, for example, British literature, counseling psychology, or twentieth-century history, and also take courses covering the entire discipline. Programs include twenty or more increasingly specialized courses and seminars plus comprehensive examinations on all major areas of the field. They also include a dissertation, which is a report that relies on original research to answer a significant question in the field, presenting an original hypothesis or proposing and testing a model.

A major step in the traditional academic career is attaining tenure. Newly hired faculty serve a certain period (usually seven years) under term contracts, at the end of which their record of teaching, research, and overall contribution to the institution is reviewed. If the review is favorable and positions are available, tenure is granted. Those denied tenure must usually leave the institution.

When a professor has tenure, he or she cannot be fired without just cause and due process. It protects the faculty's academic freedom—the ability to teach and conduct research without fear of being fired for advocating unpopular ideas. It also gives both faculty and institutions the stability needed for effective research and teaching and provides financial stability for faculty members. About 60 percent of full-time faculty are tenured, and many others are in the probationary period.

Those teaching at colleges and universities need intelligence, inquisitive and analytical minds, and a strong desire to pursue and disseminate knowledge. They must be able to communicate clearly and logically, both orally and in writing. They should be able to establish a rapport with students and, as models for them, be dedicated to the principles of academic integrity and intellectual honesty. Finally, they must be able to work in an environment where they receive little direct supervision.

Career Outlook

The career outlook for teachers varies depending on the grade level and location. Read the following section to learn more about the employment projections for the teaching field.

K–12

In the United States, job opportunities for teachers are expected to be very good through 2014, depending on the locality, grade level, and subject taught. Most openings will come from the need to replace the large number of teachers who are expected to retire during this period, as well as those who decide to leave teaching after a year or two, especially those employed in poor, urban schools. Shortages of qualified teachers will likely continue, resulting in competition among some localities.

Overall student enrollments in elementary, middle, and secondary schools are expected to rise more slowly than in the past, as children of the baby boom generation leave the school system. This will cause employment to rise between 9 and 17 percent for teachers from kindergarten through the secondary grades, depending on the region. Projected enrollments will vary by region. Fast-growing states in the West, particularly California, Idaho, Hawaii, Alaska, Utah, and New Mexico, will experience the largest enrollment increases. Enrollments in the South will increase at a more modest rate than it has in recent years, while those in the Northeast and Midwest are expected to hold relatively steady or decline. Teachers who are geographically mobile and who obtain licensure in more than one subject should have a distinct advantage in finding a job.

The job market for teachers also continues to vary by school location and by subject taught. Opportunities should be better in inner cities and rural areas than in suburban districts. Increasing enrollments of minorities, coupled with a shortage of minority teachers, should lead to increased efforts to recruit minority teachers. Also, the number of non-English-speaking students will continue to grow, which creates a demand for bilingual teachers and for those who teach English as a second language. Specialties that have an adequate number of qualified teachers include general elementary education, physical education, and social studies. Qualified vocational teachers are currently in demand in a variety of fields at both the middle- and secondary-school levels.

Prospects for teachers in Canada are expected to be good. Better government funding should increase education budgets, adding to the growth rate. The retirement rate is expected to be twice the average, and the number of retiring workers should contribute significantly to job openings, which overall should be more plentiful in rural and remote areas. Alternatively, the lower birth rate will likely weaken job growth.

An increasing number of graduates from teacher education programs will cause stiff competition for available jobs. The best prospects will be for those who develop strong research skills and stay current on issues related to their field.

College and University

Overall, employment of college and university teachers in the United States is expected to increase 27 percent or more through 2014. A significant proportion of these new jobs will be part-time positions. Job opportunities are generally expected to be very good as a number of openings for all varieties of postsecondary teachers result from the retirement of current teachers and continued increases in student enrollments.

Projected growth in college and university enrollment over the next decade stems mainly from the expected increase in the population of eigteen- to twenty-year-olds, and from the increasing number of high school graduates who choose to attend these institutions. Adults looking to expand their career opportunities are returning to college; this will continue to create new opportunities for postsecondary teachers, particularly at community colleges and for-profit institutions that are particulary attractive to working adults.

Prospects should be favorable for Ph.D. recipients seeking jobs as postsecondary teachers. While competition will remain tight for tenure-track positions at four-year colleges and universities, a considerable number of part-time or renewable term appointments will be available at these institutions and positions at community colleges. Opportunities for master's degree holders are also expected to be favorable, based on expected growth in community colleges and other institutions, such as professional career education programs.

Opportunities for graduate teaching assistants are expected to be very good because of prospects for much higher undergraduate enrollments along with more modest graduate enrollment increases. Constituting almost 9 percent of all postsecondary teachers, graduate teaching assistants play an integral role in the postsecondary education system, and they are expected to continue to do so in the future.

Job prospects for postsecondary teachers in Canada are expected to be good. Employment growth is above average because of increased government spending on education and research, and retiring workers are contributing additional job openings. Competition should be strong from recent graduates and immigrants. As demand for online education continues to grow, building computer skills will give a person a competitive edge.

Students attend postsecondary institutions to prepare themselves for careers. So the best job prospects for postsecondary teachers in the United States and Canada are likely to be in fields where job growth is expected to be strong over the next decade. These will include fields such as business, health specialties, nursing, and biological sciences. Community colleges and other institutions offering career and technical education have been among the most rapidly growing, and these institutions are expected to offer some of the best opportunities for postsecondary teachers.

Earnings

The following section provides information on salaries for teachers at various levels.

K–12

According to the American Federation of Teachers, beginning U.S. teachers with a bachelor's degree earned an average of $31,704 in the 2003–04 school year. The estimated average salary of all public elementary- and secondary-school teachers in the 2003–04 school year was $46,597. Private school teachers typically earn less than public school teachers, but they may be given other benefits, such as free or subsidized housing. In 2004, more than half of all elementary-, middle-, and secondary-school teachers belonged to unions, mainly the American Federation of Teachers and the National Education Association, which bargain with school systems over wages, hours, and other terms and conditions of employment.

According to the Canadian Teachers' Federation, teacher salaries in Canada are generally based on a combination of years of postsecondary education and years of experience. Additional allowances are paid to teachers with administrative responsibilities. Minimum entry-level salary (four or five years of postsecondary education, depending on the jurisdiction) ranges from C$34,000 to C$52,000 annually. The maximum salary for the same levels of training ranges from C$50,000 to C$72,000 annually, depending on the jurisdiction. Teachers without degrees earn lower salaries; those with advanced training and degrees are paid higher salaries.

Teachers in both countries can boost their salary in a number of ways. In some schools, teachers receive extra compensation for coaching sports and working with students in extracurricular activities. Earning a master's degree or national certification often results in a raise in pay, as does being a mentor. Some teachers earn extra income during the summer by teaching summer school or performing other jobs in the school system.

College and University

Earnings for college faculty vary according to rank and type of institution, geographic area, and field. According to a 2004–05 survey by the American Association of University Professors, salaries for full-time faculty averaged $68,505. By rank, the average was $91,548 for professors, $65,113 for associate professors, $54,571 for assistant professors, $39,899 for instructors, and $45,647 for lecturers. Faculty in four-year institutions earn higher salaries, on average, than do those in two-year schools. In 2004–05, faculty salaries averaged $79,342 in private independent institutions, $66,851 in public institutions, and $61,103 in religiously affiliated private colleges and universities.

Based on a 2003–04 survey by Statistics Canada, salaries of postsecondary teachers vary according to institution and location. Salaries for full professors range from $84,000 to more than $107,000; for associate professors, from $69,000 to $86,000; and for assistant professors, from $55,000 to $68,000.

Postsecondary teachers in both the United States and Canada who specialize in fields with high-paying nonacademic alternatives, such as medicine, law, engineering, and business, among others, generally have earnings that exceed the averages. In other fields, such as the humanities and education, they are lower.

Many faculty members obtain significant earnings in addition to their base salary, from consulting, teaching additional courses, research, writing for publication, or other employment. In addition, many college and university faculty enjoy some unique benefits, including access to campus facilities, tuition waivers for dependents, housing and travel allowances, and paid sabbatical leaves. Part-time faculty usually have fewer benefits than full-time faculty.

Strategies for Finding the Jobs

How you go about your job hunt depends, in part, on the type of job and job setting you are seeking. Here are some general suggestions.

The *Chronicle of Higher Education*
Employers advertise job openings at community colleges and four-year colleges and universities in this weekly publication. It is available by subscription or at your library or university career placement office.

Surf the Web
Most public and private schools, as well as colleges and universities, have Web pages and list current openings. You can also search school districts and gather information about different localities to compare qualifications and salaries.

The following is a list of helpful websites that post teaching and teaching-related job opportunities:

• **Academic Employment Network.** Educational employment opportunities for teachers and other school-related positions at all academic levels are listed on this site. Visit academploy.com.

- **Academic360.** Search through listings of educational institutions, faculty positions by discipline, and administrative positions by function in the United States and Canada, at academic360.com.
- **American Association of Community Colleges Career Center.** Positions for two-year community colleges are listed here, from president and dean through faculty to administration. Visit aacc.nche.edu/careerline.
- **ApplyToTeach.** Search job postings from all Canadian school boards, in addition to private schools and other employers, at applytoteach.ca.
- **The *Chronicle of Higher Education*.** Find job announcements for both faculty and staff positions from the *Chronicle's* job listings, news and information about the academic community, and excellent lists of links to other academic job resources online. Visit http://chronicle.com/jobs.
- **Education Canada.** This website focuses on jobs in the field of education in Canada. Search all locations by specialty or by province at http://educationcanada.com.
- **HigherEdJobs.** Search for a faculty or staff position by category (such as administrative, executive, or faculty) or location in the United States and Canada. Visit higheredjobs.com.
- **Jobs in Education.** The site lists available jobs in elementary schools, secondary schools, postsecondary institutions, and educational administrative offices throughout Canada. Visit jobsineducation.com.
- **The Adjunct Advocate.** Print and online magazine for adjunct faculty. The website lists a searchable database of jobs and tips for job seekers, at adjunctadvocate.com.
- **National Educators Employment Review.** Search for U.S. teaching jobs and information about certification at thereview.com.
- **NationJob.** Jobs are listed in education, from kindergarten through college, at nationjob.com/education
- **UniversityJobs.com.** Search for faculty and staff positions at colleges and universities in the United States, Canada, and other countries at ujobs.com.

Related Occupations

Besides teaching, there are other career opportunities open to liberal arts majors with education backgrounds.

K–12

Kindergarten, elementary-, and secondary-school teaching require a wide variety of skills and aptitudes, including a talent for working with children; organizational, administrative, and record-keeping abilities; research and communication skills; the power to influence, motivate, and train others; patience; and creativity.

Positions in other occupations require some of these aptitudes. Examples of related occupations include college and university faculty, counselors, education administrators, employment interviewers, librarians, preschool workers, public relations specialists, sales representatives, social workers, and trainers and employee development specialists.

College and University

College and university faculty function as both teachers and researchers. They communicate information and ideas. Related occupations include elementary- and secondary-school teachers, librarians, writers, consultants, lobbyists, trainers and employee development specialists, and policy analysts.

Faculty research activities often are similar to those of scientists, project managers, and administrators in industry, government, and nonprofit research organizations.

Professional Associations

Information on teacher certification, unions, and education-related issues may be obtained from the following organizations:

American Federation of Teachers
555 New Jersey Ave. NW
Washington, DC 20001
aft.org

Canadian Education Association
317 Adelaide St. W., Suite 300
Toronto, ON M5V 1P9
Canada
cea-ace.ca

Canadian Teachers' Federation
2490 Don Reid Dr.
Ottawa, ON K1H 1E1
Canada
ctf-fce.ca

National Board for Professional Teaching Standards
1525 Wilson Blvd., Suite 500
Arlington, VA 22209
nbpts.org

National Education Association
1201 16th St. NW
Washington, DC 20036-3290
nea.org

A list of institutions with accredited teacher education programs can be obtained from the following:

Education Canada Network
#305-478 Bernard Ave.
Kelowna, BC V1Y 6N7
Canada
http://resource.educationcanada.com/certification.html

National Council for Accreditation of Teacher Education
2010 Massachusetts Ave. NW, Suite 500
Washington, DC 20036
ncate.org

For information on becoming a teacher, alternative routes to certification, and teacher education programs, contact the following:

Education Resources Information Center (ERIC)
ERIC Project
c/o Computer Sciences Corporation
655 15th Street NW, Suite 500
Washington, DC 20005
eric.ed.gov

Information on colleges and universities is as follows:

American Association of Community Colleges
1 Dupont Circle NW, Suite 410
Washington, DC 20036
aacc.nche.edu

American Association of University Professors (AAUP)
1012 Fourteenth St. NW, Suite 500
Washington, DC 20005-3465
aaup.org

Association of Canadian Community Colleges
1223 Michael St. N., Suite 200
Ottawa, ON K1J 7T2
Canada
accc.ca

Association of Universities and Colleges of Canada
350 Albert St., Suite 600
Ottawa, ON K1R 1B1
Canada
aucc.ca

Canadian Association of University Teachers
2705 Queensview Dr.
Ottawa, ON K2B 8K2
Canada
caut.ca

7

Path 2: Corporate Communications

Words, messages, and information bombard us every day—oral, written, televised, faxed, phoned, and sent electronically. We are informed, advised, persuaded, influenced, motivated, directed, helped, entertained—and sometimes annoyed—by all the communication that confronts us. However we may feel about it, there's no escaping it. In school, at work, and at home, we constantly receive and exchange information. Professors strive to stimulate their students; bosses hope to keep their employees motivated and productive; advertisers and solicitors cram our mailboxes full of notices, advertisements, and enticements to buy or act; the telephone, television, radio, newspapers, books, and magazines all vie for our attention; and ads, surveys, and special offers flood our e-mail in-boxes. It's been reported that we spend 39 percent of all available hours within an entire year watching television, reading, and talking on the telephone. This means we spend 58 percent of our waking hours engaged in these media-oriented activities.

Although some may resent the constant intrusion, liberal arts majors can look at it differently. This pervasive focus on communication and information means unlimited opportunities for finding exciting and challenging work. The information industry outranks any other, and in the last four decades it has become the nucleus of North America's economy and labor force. More workers are now employed in some facet of the information industry than in any other sector. In fact, more than 50 percent of the U.S. workforce earns its living dealing with information.

Definition of the Career Path

If you take the simplest definition of communications as "getting the word out," the corporate community engages in this activity the most. In some sectors, the need to get the message out in-house is done through newsletters, memos, position papers, letters from the president, corporate training, seminars, and workshops; others need to get the message out to the public or to consumers through conventions, advertisements, publicity campaigns, community relations, or media contacts. The process of getting the word out can use the skills of just one person or employ teams of ten, fifty, or a hundred professionals. Their job titles and roles vary as much as the messages they strive to convey.

To hire competent communicators, employers look for graduates with liberal arts backgrounds rather than those with technical or job-specific training. A survey conducted by Silverstone, Greenbaum, and MacGregor and presented in their unpublished paper, "The Preferred College Graduate as Seen by the N.Y. Business Community" concluded that "they [CEOs] don't seem to want 'salesmen,' business 'intellectuals,' or 'ready-made' business executives (with an M.B.A. in hand). They do want team players who can express themselves with substance in ideas and thoughts."

The following diverse areas of specialization are typically offered in college and university communications departments:

- Advertising
- Education
- Family communication
- Forensics, argumentation, and debate
- Health communication
- Information sciences and human information systems
- Instructional development
- International and intercultural communication
- Interpersonal and small group interaction
- Interpretation and performance studies
- Journalism
- Legal communication
- Mass communication
- Media and communication technologies and policy
- Organizational communication
- Political communication
- Public relations
- Radio, television, and film
- Rhetorical and communication theory
- Speech and language sciences
- Theater

Today's liberal arts majors learn a wide range of skills with just as wide a range of applications. A variety of studies, however, also show that the most important skill remains the ability to communicate effectively. The ideal communications specialist might actually be a generalist. With an understanding of how to penetrate public awareness as well as mold and respond to public opinion, communications can be public relations. With the knowledge of how to reach and influence consumers, communications can be advertising or publicity and promotion. Through the techniques of writing and editing, communications can be journalism. With problem-solving and group-management skills, communications can be corporate troubleshooting or training.

Possible Job Titles

The following list gives you an idea of the scope of jobs available in the corporate world. There is much overlap across occupations and job settings. For example, job titles within the field of public relations are also found in health communications, and job titles that exist in a corporate setting also find homes within advertising agencies and marketing firms. For ease in locating particular job titles, the list has been arranged alphabetically. However, this list is by no means exhaustive. You can use this list as a reference during your job search, adding to it as you come across notices for other jobs that mention related skills.

Alumni relations coordinator
Business development manager
Civic affairs representative
Communications consultant
Communications specialist
Community affairs coordinator
Community relations specialist
Consumer affairs specialist
Copyeditor
Copywriter
Corporate communications director
Corporate communicator
Director of development
Editor
Educational affairs director

Employee publications specialist
Event coordinator
Fund-raiser
Government relations
Group/regional manager
Group/regional manager
Industrial public relations executive
Intercultural communications specialist
Intercultural communicator
Interpersonal communicator
Investor relations director
Management supervisor
Patient advocate
Press secretary
Promotional campaign developer
Public information officer
Public relations assistant
Public relations manager
Public relations writer
Research assistant
Researcher
Spokesperson
Staff writer
Volunteer coordinator

Modern public relations includes the following job titles:

Community liaison
Consultant
Corporate communicator
Corporate trainer
Government mediator
Intercultural communicator
Investor relations specialist
Media coordinator
Public information officer
Spokesperson

The following is an actual job advertisement for an experienced corporate communicator.

Senior Employee: Communications Specialist. One of America's ten best employers is seeking a well-rounded corporate communicator. The qualified applicant will be able to plan communication strategies, lead a writing team, edit and write for nationally recognized publications, and serve internal clients. Requirements include a degree in communications, journalism, or another related liberal arts field and five to ten years' corporate agency/newspaper experience to include heavy business writing. Must possess excellent skills in production and project management, communication planning, editing, writing, and interpersonal and client relations. Experience in managing print budgets and desktop publishing would be preferred.

Excellent benefits, competitive salary, and a retirement plan.

Possible Employers

Communications professionals can find positions with a wide variety of employers. Aside from corporations, the following are employment options for communications specialists:

- Communications consulting firms
- Educational institutions
- Government/military
- Labor unions
- Management consulting firms
- Nonprofit associations
- Self-employed/freelance
- State-owned corporations
- Utility companies
- Writing/editing firms

The specific industries employing communications professionals within these fields include the following:

Advertising
Aerospace
Agriculture
Audiovisual
Automotive
Chemical

Computers
Construction
Design
Education
Engineering
Finance/banking
Food/beverage
Graphic arts/printing
Hotel/lodging
Insurance
Manufacturing
Medical/health
Metals/mining
Petroleum
Pharmaceutical
Photography
Professional services
Public relations
Publishing
Real estate
Retail sales
Transportation
Utilities

Corporations

Many large corporations hire communications specialists in the human resources department. Some corporations also have specific communications departments. In addition, communications specialists are commonly found in other departments such as advertising, publications, public relations, research and development, and sales.

Private Consulting Firms

More and more private consulting firms are fulfilling communications needs for those corporations that do not choose, whether because of size or budget, to hire a permanent staff of corporate communicators, trainers, or public relations professionals. Private consulting firms work with clients on a fee-for-service basis or on a retainer. When need or problems arise, a corporation can bring in a consulting firm, first to conduct a needs analysis and then to submit a written proposal covering how they plan to proceed and how much it will cost. Consultants employed by a firm can work on a straight salary basis or for a salary plus commission.

Private Public Relations Firms

The practice of public relations is a relatively young field, formally founded less than one hundred years ago. Early definitions emphasized public relations as press agentry and publicity. As the profession evolved, those aspects became less the work of the public relations professional and fall more into the realm of publicity, advertising, and marketing professionals.

Today, public relations is a huge umbrella under which many job titles and professional responsibilities exist. The number of professionals in public relations in the United States is estimated to be more than 200,000. They are employed in every sector, from the corporate world to the sporting world, from government departments to health and medical facilities. And though the settings might vary, their main responsibility usually doesn't. The backbone of every public relations professional's job description is the role of communicator.

The public relations professional focuses on how the company is perceived by its various audiences, and he or she can also help shape a company and the way it performs. By research and evaluation, the public relations practitioner determines the expectations and concerns of the public and reports these findings back to the organization. A good public relations program needs the support of the organization and the public it is involved with.

Public relations firms function much the way private consulting firms do. They take on a variety of different clients, from large corporations to church groups and government bodies; assess their needs; propose a plan of action; and often implement that plan. Most public relations firms are located in major cities and have a staff ranging from fewer than a dozen workers to those with more than a thousand. Some workers are generalists; others specialize in specific areas such as government relations, employee communications, or educational and social programs.

Self-Employed or Freelancers

Self-employed or freelance communications consultants work similarly to their counterparts employed by private firms. The advantage is that the money earned goes directly to the consultant and not into the firm's coffer. The disadvantage is that the independent consultant has to cover all of his or her own expenses and build up a client base from scratch.

Foreign Service

The foreign services of the United States and Canada are natural choices for liberal arts majors interested in business and intercultural communications. The two foreign services offer opportunities in several areas of specialization.

U.S. Foreign Service

• **Administration.** Administrative personnel at overseas posts are responsible for hiring foreign national workers, providing office and residential space, ensuring reliable communications with Washington, D.C., supervising computer systems, and providing security for a post's personnel and property.

• **Consular services.** Consular workers must be excellent communicators and often combine the skills of lawyers, judges, investigators, and social workers. Their duties range from issuing passports and visas to finding a lost child or helping a traveler in trouble.

• **Economic officers.** Economic officers maintain contact with key business and financial leaders in the host country. They report to Washington, D.C., on the local economic conditions and their impact on American trade and investment policies. They are concerned with issues such as commercial aviation safety, fishing rights, and international banking.

• **Political affairs.** Those working in political affairs analyze and report on the political views of the host country. They make contact with labor unions, humanitarian organizations, educators, and cultural leaders.

• **Information and cultural affairs.** As part of the foreign service, the U.S. Information Agency (USIA) promotes U.S. cultural, informational, and public diplomacy programs. An information officer might develop a library open to the public, meet with the press, and oversee English-language training programs for the host country.

• **Commercial and business services.** In this division, a foreign service officer identifies overseas business connections for American exporters and investors, conducts market research for the success of U.S. products, and organizes trade shows and other promotional events.

Canadian Foreign Service

• **Management and consular affairs officers.** These officers work at Canadian diplomatic missions overseas, providing assistance to Canadians abroad in cases such as incarceration, theft, death, medical evacuation, natural disaster, loss of passport, child abduction, civil unrest, an airline crash, and so on. Those working at the Ottawa headquarters manage the area management offices that have direct budgetary and human resources authority. They brief and keep senior management informed on issues including budget transfers between corporate units and departments. They interpret and implement departmental priorities.

• **Trade commissioners.** The Trade Commissioner Service provides advice to Canadian clients on doing business in a global marketplace. This network of international business development and trade policy professionals numbers approximately 1,000 located across Canada and in 150 locations around the world. A trade commissioner must be able to adapt to ever-changing cultural, economic, and technological environments, and must also be client-service oriented, be a self-starter, and demonstrate the initiative to seek out new contacts.

- **Political/economic officers.** This job varies depending on location. At some posts, officers promote Canada's peace-building and democratic development initiatives; at other posts, the emphasis may be on negotiating an audiovisual cooperation agreement that will enhance the cultural links between countries. Officers meet and work with their international counterparts and oversee the fair running of elections, assist in brokering peace agreements between disputing factions, and advance Canada's policies on international crime and terrorism.
- **Foreign affairs immigration officers.** Those who are stationed overseas work closely with local staff, making decisions on the visa applications of visitors, students, and temporary workers. They may prepare and present briefings for headquarters, other visa offices, and partner organizations on migration issues or the social, cultural, and economic situation of the country where they are assigned. Those who work at the Ottawa headquarters provide operational support to the overseas staff. Some officers may analyze or develop strategies for dealing with financial or administrative issues. Others become involved in developing programs and policies on sponsored relatives, students, visitors, and temporary workers, or they prepare memos to the minister, setting out and justifying proposed policy changes.

Although many foreign service officers are skilled in political science and history, candidates are expected to have knowledge in specialized fields such as communications, the environment, computer science, and trade.

Government Agencies

You may not initially connect working for government agencies with corporate communications. However, the services the government needs are similar, if not identical to, those used in the business world. Internal employee relations and external public relations are concerns as important in the public sector as they are in the private sector. Although the job titles might vary—that is, public information officer rather than public relations specialist—the services they perform are the same.

In addition to the foreign service, many government agencies and departments at the local, state, and federal levels use the services of professional communicators.

Military

The military use both civilian and noncivilian personnel in a variety of communications activities, from promotion and recruitment to public information and intelligence. Public information officers (PIOs) deal with the community, the media, and internal communications, usually in the form of base newsletters or other military publications. Both at home and abroad, intelligence agencies employ communications specialists who are expert in gathering data and channeling it to the appropriate offices.

A stint in military communications can be a career in itself or an excellent stepping-stone to the corporate world.

Utilities

Utility companies no longer sit quietly in the background going about their business of providing power. Environmentalists (or rather the public relations professionals who work for them) have raised public awareness about the dangers of potential and existing environmental hazards. Public relations professionals employed by utilities keep communication open, instituting programs to work with the community, and documenting and explaining their impact on the environment.

Communications majors in this field need to be skilled negotiators and as comfortable with a computer as with a microphone.

Labor Unions

Labor unions recognize the importance of building support for their programs and positions. Major unions and their affiliates operate news and speaker bureaus; publish a variety of newsletters, reports, brochures, and other materials; and offer educational programs to civic groups and schools.

A liberal arts major can find a satisfying career in this setting.

Nonprofit Associations

The term *nonprofit* refers to a tax status that exempts some organizations from partial or complete tax payments; it never was intended to mean that a profit couldn't be made. Having said that, it is true that the nonprofit sector often has less money (and more need for it) than the private, profit-making sector. Salaries in these settings might be lower, however, the work experience can be equally, if not more, rewarding than in the corporate world.

Hundreds of thousands of nonprofit associations—including charitable organizations, private foundations, professional associations, and some educational institutions—exist throughout Canada and the United States. Charitable groups such as Easter Seals, the American Red Cross, the American Cancer Society, Canadian Red Cross, Canadian Cancer Society, Big Brothers/Big Sisters, the United Way, YMCA and YWCA, Boy Scouts of America, Girl Guides of Canada, the American Heart Association, and others all need employees with strong communications skills. For every profession, there is at least one professional association, a membership-supported organization that joins groups of people with common interests and career goals. Most new graduates look upon professional associations as a resource for career support and help with finding a job; communications majors realize that this setting can be the ultimate career goal in itself.

Specialist communicators working for charitable organizations and professional associations perform much the same functions as their counterparts in the corporate world. Promotional campaigns need to be developed, media contacts have to be made, and employee and community relations need to be maintained. Add fund-raising and membership drives to this mix.

Growth in this sector seems to be on the rise, and more and more rewarding opportunities are becoming available.

Hospitals and Medical Centers

The health-care industry—and it is indeed an industry—has a growing need for communications specialists in much the same capacity as the corporate world. With changes in national health care policies, the need for specialists in public relations, community affairs, marketing, and other related areas is increasing.

Possible settings include the following:

- Government-funded agencies (such as the Centers for Disease Control or Canadian Institutes of Health)
- Health advertising agencies
- Hospitals (both private and community based)
- Outpatient medical centers
- Pharmaceutical companies
- Professional schools of medicine
- Rehabilitation clinics
- Residential treatment facilities
- Volunteer health organizations

Job titles and responsibilities are similar to those in the corporate world. The main skill being sought is the ability to communicate effectively.

Higher Education

Universities, colleges, and other educational institutions have a great need for liberal arts majors from a variety of backgrounds. Here are just a few departments in which you would be qualified to work:

- Admissions—communicating the highlights of the institution to attract new students
- Alumni relations—maintaining contact with alumni for the purpose of fund-raising and community relations
- Career placement and service centers—establishing contact with potential employees and providing career counseling and guidance to students
- Community affairs/relations—ensuring open communication and cooperation between the institution and neighboring community, and developing outreach programs that provide adult and continuing-education programs
- Cooperative education—maintaining contact with the business community and other fields for student job placement
- Development—continuing the ongoing process of fund-raising, targeting other groups in addition to alumni
- International student affairs—providing orientation, counseling, and help with immigration procedures to foreign students
- Publications—working with campus newspapers, magazines, college catalogs, yearbooks, and other print needs of the institution

Working Conditions

Corporations, public relations firms, and most of the possible employers explored in this chapter are usually busy, hectic places. Deadlines need to be met, phones are ringing, visitors are arriving, and work schedules are being interrupted frequently. Public relations professionals and all the other corporate communicators put in long, sometimes irregular hours. Once a project is under way or a crisis needs to be resolved, the work seldom stops until the job is done.

Employees of nonprofit corporations, associations, and charitable organizations generally enjoy a calmer, though not pressure-free, work atmosphere. These organizations have the same need for effective communicators but have a lot less money to accomplish their goals.

Workloads in different settings vary, too. You can be hired to conduct a weeklong workshop on effective speaking and listening skills designed particularly for a phone company. Then when you're finished, there's the company report to work on, letters to write, phone calls to return, meetings to attend, and research to be done. The pace can be exhilarating and challenging to some, stress-producing to others.

Training and Qualifications

A bachelor's degree in communications, English, or a related liberal arts major provides a good entry for any of the fields covered in this chapter. While some positions, such as assistant/junior copywriters, don't require a four-year degree, a bachelor of arts or even a master's degree will give you an edge as the competition for jobs increases. But a degree alone isn't sufficient. You need a host of skills to supplement your educational training to have a successful career in communications. The following skills have been identified by communications professionals as among those most commonly used:

Audience research
Audiovisual production
Budgeting/cost control
Communication planning
Event planning
Feature writing
Feedback system design
Film production
Government relations
Graphic design
Investor relations
Magazine layout
Management skills
Media contact
Newsletter editing
Newswriting
Personnel supervision
Print production
Proposal writing
Scriptwriting
Speech writing
Time management

The more skills you are able to acquire or develop, the better your chances of securing the type of job you are seeking. The following skills and personal qualities become important depending upon the area of business communications you choose to pursue.

Bilingual or multilingual abilities
Compassion
Creativity
Cross-cultural sensitivity
Detail-oriented skills
Drive
Empathy
Judgment
Initiative
Integrity
Intelligence
Interpersonal skills
Organizational skills
Research skills
Verbal skills
Writing skills

You may have been born with some of these qualities; others can be learned. Future communications specialists can start while in college. In addition to courses required for the major, a host of other classes will enrich your skill bank and enhance your résumé. These days, with more and more businesses and organizations entering the international marketplace, being fluent in one or more foreign languages can only work in your favor. Enroll in classes in economics, finance, management, sociology, psychology, and public speaking.

Get as much practical hands-on experience as you can while in college. Work for the student newspaper or on the yearbook staff. Help organize student activities, volunteer for the speakers' bureau, or become a peer counselor. Participate in work-study or cooperative education programs, and take advantage of any internships or practicums you can line up, even if it means extending your graduation date a semester.

Most university programs work with local, national, and sometimes international businesses to place students in hands-on internships. If your university does not have access to these types of placements, try to arrange one on your own. An inquiry directed to the right company could be all it takes to open the door to a rewarding experience.

Many successful communications specialists also have a record of volunteer service with civic groups and charities. For those seeking intercultural experiences, find summer employment overseas or do a stint in the Peace

Corps after graduation. Teaching English as a foreign language is a rewarding way to acquire cross-cultural experience. While on campus, interact with the international student office or volunteer in the English as a second language (ESL) program. Intercultural sensitivity and experience is difficult to gain just in the classroom.

The job market is competitive, but it is open to newcomers, especially to those who have shown initiative in preparing themselves as much as possible.

Career Outlook

Corporate communications should continue to be a growing field, with keen competition expected for entry-level public relations jobs, as the number of qualified applicants is expected to exceed the number of job openings. Many are attracted to this profession because the nature of the work is high profile. Opportunities should be best for college graduates who combine a degree in journalism, public relations, advertising, or another communications-related field with a public relations internship or other related work experience. Applicants who do not have the appropriate educational background or work experience will face the toughest obstacles.

The need for strong corporate communications in an increasingly competitive business environment should spur demand for communications specialists in organizations of all types and sizes. The value of a company is measured not just by its balance sheet, but also by the strength of its relationships with those it depends on for its success. With the increasing demand for corporate accountability, more emphasis will be placed on improving the image of the client, as well as on building public confidence.

Job seekers looking for the highly coveted positions as communications managers will face stiff competition. College graduates with related experience, a high level of creativity, and strong communication skills should have the best job opportunities. In particular, employers are looking for those who have the computer skills to conduct advertising, marketing, promotions, public relations, and sales activities on the Internet.

Earnings

In 2004, the median annual earnings for salaried public relations specialists were $43,830. The majority earned between $32,970 and $59,360, while the lowest 10 percent earned less than $25,750, and the top 10 percent earned more than $81,120. Median earnings in the industries employing the largest numbers of public relations specialists were as follows: advertising and related services, $50,450; management of companies and enterprises, $47,330; business, professional, labor, political, and similar organizations, $45,400; local government, $44,550; and colleges, universities, and professional schools, $39,610.

Strategies for Finding the Jobs

There are a half million active corporations in the United States and Canada. While not every one provides a setting where a communications major would prefer to work, enough do.

• **Scan the help-wanted ads.** The traditional job-hunting method—reviewing help-wanted ads—seldom reaps rewards for the new, inexperienced grad. Most job advertisements are for specialists with time and experience under their belts, or for pre-entry-level clerical jobs that might not offer enough exposure to lead to promotion. However, this doesn't mean that you should ignore the want ads. The job you are perfect for could suddenly appear in next Sunday's paper. Search the Internet for an even wider base of advertised positions. Sites such as monster.com and careerbuilder.com post thousands of available positions.

• **Knock on doors.** Knocking on doors is what experts advise. Find the firm for which you would like to work, and become a familiar face in the personnel department or front reception area.

• **Join professional associations.** Professional associations often maintain job banks, and the journals and newsletters they publish usually feature job advertisements. Their regional or national conferences usually have job clearinghouses with recruiters in attendance.

• **Find a mentor.** Your alumni association can put you in touch with professionals who might be willing to help you. In addition to helping you locate job leads, a mentor can help you present your most professional self to potential employers.

• **Check with your college department.** Don't forget to inquire at your college communications department office. It is not unusual for a corporation to call a university and ask for a list of graduating seniors. The jobs they are seeking to fill might also be announced on department bulletin boards.

• **Register with your college placement office.** College placement offices or college career service centers can also provide good leads for your job search. While some employers contact individual departments directly, others send their job openings to the placement office or career counselor.

Related Occupations

The skills that liberal arts majors possess are valued in a number of related professions. The following is a small sampling of occupations that draw on similar skills to a greater or lesser degree.

Biocommunications
Development specialist
Financial manager
Health science communications
Industrial psychologist
In-house legal counsel
Lobbyist
Medical writer
Technical writer
Volunteer coordinator

Help in Locating Employers

Search the Internet. Countless websites can help you locate job opportunities. In particular, check out the Job Center page for the Public Relations Society of America (PRSA) at prsa.org/jobcenter. In addition to an overview of public relations careers, you'll find places to post your résumé or classified ad.

Visit the library, where many directories list professional associations, public relations firms, and corporations by industry. Make friends with your reference librarian, and bring plenty of change for the copy machine. The following contacts, journals, and directories only begin to scratch the surface:

American Communication Journal
American Communication Association
americancomm.org

Canadian Foreign Service
Enquiries Service (SXCI)
Foreign Affairs Canada
125 Sussex Dr.
Ottawa, ON K1A 0G2
Canada
international.gc.ca

Canadian Journal of Communication
cjc-online.ca

Communication World
International Association of Business Communicators
1 Hallidie Plaza, Suite 600
San Francisco, CA 94102
iabc.com

Encyclopedia of Associations
Thomson Gale
gale.com

Investor Relations Guide
Kennedy Information
1 Phoenix Mill Ln., 3rd Floor
Peterborough, NH 03458
kennedyinfo.com/ir

O'Dwyer's Directory of Corporate Communications
O'Dwyer's Directory of Public Relations Firms
Public Relations News
J.R. O'Dwyer Company, Inc.
271 Madison Ave.
New York, NY 10016
odwyerpr.com

Peace Corps Recruitment
peacecorp.gov

Public Relations Review
Elsevier
elsevier.com

Public Relations Strategist
Public Relations Tactics
Public Relations Society of America
33 Maiden Ln., 11th Floor
New York, NY 10038-5150
prsa.org

Speechwriter's Newsletter
Lawrence Ragan Communications, Inc.
111 East Wacker Dr., Suite 500
Chicago, IL 60601
ragan.com

U.S. Foreign Service
U.S. Department of State
HR/REE/REC
2401 E St. NW, Suite 518 H
Washington, DC 20522
careers.state.gov

Professional Associations

The following list shows the variety of professional associations active in the world of business communications. Most offer booklets and pamphlets for free or for a very nominal charge. Many of the associations provide job placement services and publish career-oriented journals and magazines. Visit their websites or send them an e-mail or note for more information.

American Advertising Federation
1101 Vermont Ave. NW, Suite 500
Washington, DC 20005-6306
aaf.org
Services: Training, internships, conferences, awards, competitions

American Association of Advertising Agencies
405 Lexington Ave., 18th Floor
New York, NY 10174-1801
aaaa.org
Services: Job postings, conferences, training

American Business Women's Association
9100 Ward Pkwy.
PO Box 8728
Kansas City, MO 64114-0728
abwahq.org
Services: conferences, awards

American Society for Training and Development
1640 King St.
Box 1443
Alexandria, VA 22313-2043
astd.org
Services: Job bank, career information, training, seminars, workshops, publications

Association for Business Communication
businesscommunication.org
Services: Job board, publications, conventions, awards

The Association for Women in Communications
3337 Duke St.
Alexandria, VA 22314
womcom.org
Services: Publications, annual conference, placement service, career information

Canadian Advertising Research Foundation
160 Bloor St. E., Suite 1005
Toronto, ON M4W 1B9
Canada
carf.ca
Services: Newsletter, seminars, courses

Canadian Communication Association
acc-cca.ca
Services: Publications, conference, awards

Canadian Federation of Independent Businesses
cfib.ca
Services: Online courses, newsletter, surveys

Canadian Public Relations Society
4195 Dundas St. W., Suite 346
Toronto, ON M8X 1Y4
Canada
cprs.ca
Services: Professional development, awards, conference

Canadian Society for Training and Development
720 Spadina Ave., Suite 315
Toronto, ON M5S 2T9
Canada
cstd.ca
Services: Certification, conferences, publications, job bank, awards

Health and Science Communications Association
39 Wedgewood Dr., Suite A
Jewett City, CT 06351
hesca.org
Services: Annual conference, local and regional meetings, publications, job placement services

Institute for Public Relations
PO Box 118400
Gainesville, FL 32611-8400
instituteforpr.com
Services: Research, annual lectures, competitions, publications

International Association of Business Communicators
1 Hallidie Plaza, Suite 600
San Francisco, CA 94102
iabc.com
Services: Career and job postings, publications, conferences

International Communication Association
1500 21st St. NW
Washington, DC 20036
icahdq.org
Services: Conferences, publications

International Labor Communications Association
815 16th St. NW, Four North
Washington, D.C. 20006
ilcaonline.org
Services: Job listings, publications

International Listening Association
listen.org
Services: Conventions, publications

National Business Association
PO Box 700728
Dallas, TX 75370
nationalbusiness.org
Services: Publications, scholarships

National Communication Association
1765 N. St. NW
Washington, DC 20036
natcom.org
Services: Annual convention, conferences, publications, awards, job placement

National Council for Marketing and Public Relations
PO Box 336039
Greeley, CO 80633
ncmpr.org
Services: Annual conference, publications

Public Relations Society of America
33 Maiden Ln., 11th Floor
New York, NY 10038-5150
prsa.org
Services: Training, publications, job listings

Religious Communication Association
Department of Communication
The University of Texas at Tyler
3900 University Blvd.
Tyler, TX 75799
americanrhetoric.com
Services: Conferences, workshops, scholarships, seminars, publications

8

Path 3: Media

The United States supports the largest mass media system of any country in the world, which has generated millions of jobs throughout North America. The options for liberal arts majors in search of great jobs in this area could be daunting if it weren't so exciting.

The field of journalism is perhaps the most traditional path open to English and communications majors within liberal arts or general studies programs. The fourth estate no longer refers only to newspapers; this ever expanding field includes syndicates and wire services, television and radio, consumer and trade publications, and the Internet. While these outlets provide a home for journalists to report and interpret the news, they also create niches for creative writers with a vast array of specialties, as well as for editors, agents, entertainers, broadcasters, producers, photographers, computer experts, and other important frontline and support positions.

Definition of the Career Path

Because the range of jobs within the media is so vast and many positions are found in several different outlets, it is more efficient to examine each outlet as its own career path. For example, while the role of editor will vary depending on the setting, many of the same functions and skills are used for newspapers as well as for magazines. The definitive question is not whether to become an editor, but to decide in which environment you will be most satisfied. Similarly, a liberal arts major with hopes of becoming a writer will benefit from knowing the types of assignments and working conditions involved at the different job settings or whether a career as a freelancer is a viable alternative. Be assured that for every interest a liberal arts major has, there is a job and a setting to satisfy it.

Possible Job Titles

Job titles within the media cover the range of writers, editors, entertainers, production workers, and a host of other professionals employed in departments not covered in this chapter. The following list is not meant to be exhaustive. Look for additional related job titles and descriptions in other chapters in this book. Also, *The Dictionary of Occupational Titles* (U.S. Department of Labor) gives a comprehensive list with generic descriptions.

Print Media
Acquisitions editor
Art director
Assignment editor
Assistant editor
Associate editor
Author
Book editor
Bureau chief
Bureau reporter
City editor
Columnist
Contracts assistant
Copyeditor
Copywriter
Correspondent
Critic
Desk assistant
Dramatic agent
Editor
Editorial writer
Editor in chief
Electronic publishing specialist
Executive editor
External publications editor
Feature writer
Freelance editor
Freelance writer

Internal publications editor
Investigative reporter
Journalist
Literary agent
Managing editor
News editor
Newspaper editor
News writer
Photojournalist
Production editor
Publisher
Reporter
Researcher
Section editor
Senior editor
Senior writer
Staff writer
Story editor
Stringer
Syndicated columnist
Technical editor
Writer

Radio and Television
Announcer
Associate news director
Audiovisual manager/director
Audiovisual producer
Audiovisual technician
Audiovisual writer
Broadcast engineers
Broadcast technicians
CAD Specialist
Correspondent
Director
Disc jockey
Filmmaker
First assistant director
Graphics coordinator
Media resource director

Mixer
Music director
Music librarian
News announcer
Newscaster
News director
News editor
News writer
Operations manager
Production assistant
Production manager
Production sound mixer
Program manager
Public services director
Radio/TV traffic assistant
Radio/TV traffic supervisor
Scriptwriter
Station manager
TV director
TV managing editor
TV producer
TV production assistant
TV tape-film manager
Video specialist

Newspapers

Newspapers make up the largest segment of the entire publishing industry, mainly because they write much of their own material as well as typically print and even distribute their newspapers. With more than 15,000 newspapers in the United States and Canada, many employment opportunities for the liberal arts major exist in this field.

Most newspapers are usually organized around the following departments: news, editorial, advertising, production, and circulation. They all provide job opportunities for communications majors. However, for the purpose of this chapter, we will focus on the news and editorial sections.

The News Department. Two major positions in the news department are those of reporter and photojournalist.

• **Reporters.** A job as a reporter is viewed as a glamorous and exciting career; it probably attracts more applicants than any other spot on a newspaper staff. As a result, competition is stiff—reporters make up less than one-fourth of a newspaper's roster. A reporter's work is challenging and fast-paced, with the pressures of deadlines and space allotments always looming overhead. This is the ideal job for those who like to be one step ahead of the general public in knowing what's going on. Whatever the size or location of the newspaper, the reporter covers local, state, national, or international events and puts all the news together to keep the reading public informed. News reporters could be assigned to a variety of stories, from covering a major world event, to monitoring the actions of public figures, to writing about a current political campaign.

• **Photojournalists.** Photojournalism is the telling of a story through pictures. Although photographs take precedence over written copy in this form of journalism, photojournalists need to have a strong journalism background, too. To accurately report the news, whether through photographs or copy, you need to be aware of what's happening in the world and why. Being a jack-of-all-trades is a main requirement for this career. Most photojournalists who work for both major and minor newspapers are expected to cover the mundane as well as the exciting. The gamut runs from food to fashion, from spot news to sports, and includes a wide range of human-interest features.

The Editorial Department. The editorial sections of newspapers vary with size and location, but most include at least some, if not all, of the following sections:

Art
Books
Business
Consumer affairs
Court system
Crime desk
Education
Entertainment
Fashion
Foreign affairs
Finance
Food
Health
International news
Lifestyles/features
Local news

National news
Religion
Science
Social events
Sports
State news
Travel

Let's look at the key editorial positions of staff writers and section editors.

Staff or feature writers function in much the same way as news reporters but are generally assigned a regular beat, such as health and medicine, sports, travel, or consumer affairs. Working in these specialized fields, they keep the public informed about important trends or breakthroughs.

At times, some think of feature writers as working only on fluff, or inconsequential, pieces; this is definitely not the case. While staff writers assigned to areas such as fashion or entertainment might not do investigative pieces, writers assigned to health or medicine certainly can.

An example is Nancy McVicar, a senior writer for the lifestyle section of the *Sun-Sentinel* in Fort Lauderdale, Florida. Her work has been nominated several times for the Pulitzer Prize, and she has won other national awards. Nancy was the first reporter to investigate the question of whether cell phones cause any potential harm to users. Her stories were picked up by wire services and shown on the television programs "20/20" and "60 Minutes." Based on her work, the U.S. Government Accountability Office (GAO), which is also the investigative arm of Congress, was asked to do an in-depth report on whether or not cellular phones are safe. Writers in every section of a newspaper, from health to politics to local news, can find a way to make an impact.

Section editor is a very desirable position for many. Although there are exceptions, section editors have usually paid their dues as reporters or staff writers, who only after a few years of experience are eligible for consideration.

The duties involved depend in part on the section, but there are many common responsibilities. Editors write articles or supervise the work of staff writers, giving assignments, reviewing copy, and making sure attention is paid to space requirements. They also attend editorial meetings and correspond with freelance writers.

Many perks are associated with some of the sections: travel writers travel, book editors get free books in the mail to read and review, sports editors go to games, food editors eat out, society page editors are invited to a myriad of social events, and so on.

Working Conditions. Reporters and photojournalists always have deadlines looming. Fiction writers can work at their own pace, but reporters do not have the luxury of waiting for their creative juices to flow. A news reporter has to file a story, or maybe even two, by a certain time every day. Although a staff writer or section editor with a weekly column has more leeway, everything still must meet the deadline in time to go to press.

Reporters gather information by visiting the scene, interviewing people, following leads and news tips, and examining documents. They take notes or use a recording device while collecting facts. Later they organize their material, decide what the focus or emphasis should be, and then write their stories, generally using a computer. Many reporters use notebook computers, which allow them to write their stories from any location and file them electronically.

Some newspapers have modern, state-of-the-art equipment; others do not have the financing they require for this technology. A reporter could work in a comfortable, private office or in a room filled with the noise of computer printers and coworkers talking on the telephone.

Working hours vary. Some writers and editors work Monday through Friday, nine to five, while others cover evenings, nights, and weekends. On some occasions, reporters work longer-than-normal hours to cover an important ongoing story or to follow late-breaking developments.

Although some desk work is involved, newspaper reporting is definitely not a desk job. Excellent interviewing and research skills are a must and a reporter needs to be able to juggle several assignments at once. Computer and typing skills are very important, too.

A reporter also must know how to "write tight." While feature writers can be more creative, news reporters must make sure they fit all the facts within a particular amount of space. The editor might allocate only a column inch or two for your story, leaving room for just the essentials of who, what, when, where, why, and how.

Training and Qualifications. A college degree is a must and most employers prefer a B.A. in journalism or communications. Others would consider a degree in a related field such as political science or English.

Your college courses should include introductory mass media, basic reporting and copyediting, history of journalism, and press law and ethics. Involvement on a school paper or an internship at a newspaper will boost your résumé. Experience as a stringer—a part-time reporter who is paid only for stories printed—is also helpful.

If you're considering the highly competitive field of photojournalism, it's very important to have a good portfolio. Most photojournalists have at least a bachelor's degree, and many, especially those with management aspirations, have a master's.

Career Outlook. Based on a number of factors, employment of news analysts, reporters, and correspondents is expected to grow only 8 percent through the year 2014. Consolidation and convergence should continue in the publishing and broadcasting industries, allowing companies to more efficiently allocate their news analysts, reporters, and correspondents to cover stories. Constantly improving technology also is allowing workers to do their jobs more efficiently, limiting the number of workers needed to cover a story or certain type of news. The number of job openings in the newspaper and broadcasting industries is sensitive to economic ups and downs, because these industries depend on advertising revenue.

However, the continued demand for news will create some job opportunities. For example, some job growth likely will occur in newer media areas, such as online newspapers and magazines. Job openings also will emerge from the need to replace workers who leave their occupations permanently; some news analysts, reporters, and correspondents find the work too stressful and hectic or do not like the lifestyle, so they transfer to other occupations.

Competition will continue for jobs on large metropolitan and national newspapers; most job opportunities will be with small-town and suburban newspapers. Talented writers able to handle highly specialized scientific or technical subjects have an advantage. Also, newspapers increasingly are hiring stringers and freelancers.

Earnings. Salaries for news analysts, reporters, and correspondents vary widely. Median annual earnings of all reporters and correspondents were $31,320 in 2004, with the majority earning between $22,900 and $47,860. The lowest 10 percent earned less than $18,470, and the highest 10 percent earned more than $68,250. Median earnings of reporters and correspondents employed by newspapers were $30,070.

Median annual earnings of broadcast news analysts were $36,980 in 2004. The middle 50 percent earned between $25,560 and $68,440. The lowest 10 percent earned less than $19,040, and the highest 10 percent earned more than $122,800. Median annual earnings of broadcast news analysts were $37,840 in radio and television broadcasting.

Magazines

Browse any bookstore, newsstand, or the Internet, and you will see hundreds of magazines covering a variety of topics, from cooking and crafts to sports and cars. There are also many you won't see there, such as the hundreds of trade journals and magazines written for businesses, industries, and professional workers. These publications all offer information on diverse subjects to their equally diverse readership. They are filled with articles and profiles, interviews and editorials, letters and advice, as well as pages and pages of advertisements.

Positions with magazines are very similar to those found in newspapers. Whether you work for a magazine full-time or as an independent freelancer, you will discover that there is no shortage of markets where you can find work or sell your articles.

Freelance Writing

A freelance writer works independently in rented office space or in a home office. Most freelance writers plan and write articles and columns on their own and actively seek out new markets for them. Freelancers trade job security and regular pay for their independence. Staff writers for newspapers and magazines might have less freedom in what they choose to write, but they generally have more job security and always know when their next paycheck will arrive. Both freelancers and those permanently employed have to produce high-quality work. They have editors to report to and deadlines to meet.

More and more magazines are willing to work with freelancers these days. With budget cuts and staff layoffs, and because magazines don't have syndicated material to fall back on, it is generally less expensive to pay several different freelance writers by the piece, rather than employ a full-time staff writer or two.

Some freelancers are generalists who write about anything they think they can sell. Others are specialists, choosing to write only in a particular field, such as travel or health and medicine. Successful freelancers have a lot of market savvy, meaning they are familiar with all the different publications they could market their work to and know how to approach those publications.

Training. While many writers polish their writing skills while in college, the business of freelancing is generally self-taught. However, throughout the country, adult-education classes, as well as writers' associations, can provide some guidance and teach marketing techniques to new freelancers.

Before you begin, read as many magazines as you can, particularly those you would like to write for. It's never a good idea to send an article to a magazine you are unfamiliar with. Exposure to different magazines also helps you come up with future article ideas. You can find out about different magazines and the kind of material they prefer to publish in the market guides listed toward the end of this chapter.

Once you have decided what you want to write about, you can proceed in two ways. You can write the entire article on speculation, send it off to appropriate editors, and hope they like your topic. Or you can write a query letter—like a mini-proposal—to see if there is any interest in your idea. Query letters save you the time of writing articles you might have difficulty selling. You would only proceed once you're given a definite assignment.

Earnings. Getting a check for an article can be rewarding, but in reality, for new freelancers, checks might not come often enough and are not always large enough to live on. While staff writers are paid a regular salary (though generally not a very high one), a freelancer gets paid only when he or she sells an article. Fees could range from as low as $5 to $1,000 or more, depending on the publication. But even with a high-paying magazine, writers often are not paid until their story is published. Because publishers can plan issues six months or more in advance, payment could be delayed from three months to a year or more.

To the freelancer's advantage, sometimes the same article can be sold to more than one magazine or newspaper, and these resales increase income. You can also be paid additional money if you can provide your own photographs to illustrate your articles.

Freelance writers don't need a long, impressive résumé to sell their first article. The writing will speak for itself.

Publishing Houses and Literary Agencies

The busy and exciting world of publishing is filled with risks, surprises, and sometimes disappointments. Without the publishing world, writers would never see their words in print; there would be no magazines, newspapers, or books for the public to enjoy; no textbooks for students and teachers to work with; and no written sources for information on any subject. Professionals in the publishing industry determine which books and stories will see print, and to some extent, help shape the tastes of the reading public.

Publishing is a competitive business, with financial concerns often determining which books will be published. Editors and agents have to be able to recognize good writing and know what topics are popular and what will sell.

For editors, agents, and writers, nothing is more exciting than having a book you worked on finally see print and land in the bookstores. The hope is that the book will take off and find its way to the bestseller list and into the homes of thousands of readers. Then everyone can be happy, from bookstore owners to the sales team and distributors. But there are only ten to fifteen slots on the various bestseller lists, and with thousands of books published each year, the odds are against producing a blockbuster.

Some books have steady sales and can stay on the publishers' backlist for years, however, others don't do as well and can disappear from bookstore shelves after only a month or so.

Every book is a gamble; no one can ever predict what will happen. Nonetheless, successful editors and agents thrive on the excitement. In the publishing world, anything is possible. Literary agents act as go-betweens for writers and editors. Most publishing houses no longer accept manuscripts submitted directly by an author, and they will only consider those that come from an agent. Agents should be familiar with the different kinds of books that publishers prefer to take on, and they are considered qualified to screen out inappropriate submissions.

An agent spends time reading manuscripts, choosing which ones to work with, and then trying to sell them to publishers. They free a writer to concentrate on writing instead of marketing their work, as it is the agent's job to find the right house for a writer's work. Once successful, the agent negotiates the best financial deal for the writer. Agents also handle film rights for feature films or TV movies, as well as foreign rights, selling books to publishers overseas.

How Publishing Houses Are Structured. A small press that puts out only three or four books a year might operate with a staff of only two or three. In this setting each person has to wear many hats: as acquisitions editor, finding new projects to publish; as typesetter and proofreader; as sales manager; as promoter and publicist; and as clerk and secretary.

The large publishing houses, which for the most part are located in New York City, can have hundreds of employees and are separated into different departments such as editorial, contracts, legal, sales and marketing, and publicity and promotion, each with a number of different job titles. For example, the editorial department includes the positions of editorial assistant, assistant or associate editor, editor, senior editor, acquisitions editor, managing editor, production editor, executive editor, editor in chief, publisher, and president.

Editors. Editors work in book-producing publishing houses or for magazines and newspapers. They read manuscripts, talk with writers, and decide which books, stories, or articles they will publish. They must also stay current on what other houses or publications are printing, to know what's out there and what's selling.

Once a manuscript is selected for publication, an editor oversees the various steps to produce the finished product, from line editing for mistakes, to choosing the book or magazine cover art and copy. Editors also regularly attend editorial meetings and occasionally travel to writers' conferences to speak to aspiring writers and to find new talent.

How Literary Agencies Are Structured. Some literary agents choose to work on their own, with little more than administrative assistance. They can rent space in an office building or work from a home office. Others might opt to work for a literary agency, either as the owner or as one of the associates. They can still function independently, choosing the writers and book projects they want to work with. Those who work in agencies usually must contribute a percentage of their income to cover the office's operating expenses.

Training for Editors and Agents. This is an excellent field for liberal arts majors because most editors and agents have at least a bachelor's degree in communications, English, journalism, or any relevant liberal arts or humanities field. It's also helpful to be familiar with publishing law and contracts.

In publishing, rarely will someone start out as an editor or agent without any prior experience. Many agents work for publishing houses first, becoming familiar with the editorial process and contracts before moving into a literary agency. Within a publishing house, there is a distinct ladder that most editors climb as they gain experience and develop a successful track record. They usually start out as editorial assistants, answering the phone, opening and distributing the mail, and preparing correspondence. Some editorial assistants are first readers for their editors; they'll read a manuscript, and then write a reader's report. If it's a positive report, the editor will take a look at the manuscript. Most editorial assistants learn the editing process from the editor they work for, and over time they move up into editorial positions with more and more responsibility.

Earnings for Editors and Agents. Editors are generally paid a set salary. Although their salary does not depend from week to week on the sales success of the books they choose to publish, an editor with a good track record is likely to be promoted and given raises. Starting pay, however, is not particularly glamorous.

In 2004, median annual earnings for salaried editors were $43,890; most earned between $33,130 and $58,850. Median annual earnings of those working for newspaper, periodical, book, and directory publishers were $43,620.

Agents, on the other hand, must sell their clients' manuscripts to publishers in order to earn any income. Most work on a commission basis, earning generally 10 to 15 percent of the money the writer earns. An agent with a lot of market savvy and who carefully chooses which manuscripts to represent and successfully bargains for big advances and royalty percentages can make a very good living, often much more than the editors to whom he or she is selling.

However, the marketplace is fickle and trends come and go. Publishing houses merge and often decrease the number of books that will go to print. In a bad year, an agent often has to struggle to make a living.

Radio and Television Stations

The golden age of radio passed five or six decades ago, but it is still considered one of the most effective of the mass media, especially for quickly disseminating information to a large number of people. Television is equally as effective. Elizabeth Kolbert, writing about television in the *New York Times*, noted that "Television has created not so much a global village as a global front stoop. Instead of gossiping about our neighbors, about whom we know less and less, we gossip about national figures, about whom we know more and more. The color set in the den has so successfully replaced the sewing circle and the hamburger joint that we are now trying to get from television that which television has caused us to give up."

Radio and television stations provide a wide range of jobs for communications majors. Several positions such as announcers and news directors exist in both settings, and some jobs at radio stations will open otherwise closed doors at television stations. The jobs that communications majors most qualify for are announcer or disc jockey (DJ), music director, program director, production manager or public service director, news writer or editor, and scriptwriter. The duties of each job vary, depending on the format and the size of the station. For example, radio stations can offer specialized programming such as country music, oldies, all-talk shows, all-news, religious broadcasts, or a combination of programming. An all-music program would require less scheduling than an all-news station. Similarly, a DJ working for a music format station will have less preparation to do than a talk-show host would.

Announcer/DJ. This is the most visible and the most competitive position. Successful DJs build a rapport with their audience and can become well-known personalities. Talk show DJs can articulate and defend opinions on both sides of any topic. They also have an entertainer's instinct for performing.

Music Director. The music director selects and organizes prerecorded music that fits the station's format. Ideally, the music director would be a fan of and knowledgeable about the station's particular area of programming and share the taste of the listening audience. Some music directors also double as announcers.

Program Director/Production Manager/Public Service Director. In small stations one person might handle the duties of all three job titles; in larger-market stations each position has its own director. Program directors manage a staff of announcers, writers, and producers and schedule broadcasts on a day-to-day basis. A production manager makes sure that programs are aired on schedule, and a public service director determines which public service announcements best serve the needs of the community and deserve airtime.

News Writer/Editor/Director. Personnel in the news department of radio and TV stations must keep on top of breaking news such as political events, natural disasters, and social issues. Weather and traffic reports sometimes originate from this department. News specialists must have good written and oral skills and able to interview people and conduct research.

Scriptwriter. Scriptwriters prepare copy for commercials, public service announcements, and for slots between programming. The number of openings in this area is small; the most active employers of scriptwriters are radio stations that program on-air dramas and talk shows.

Earnings. Median annual earnings of reporters and correspondents in radio broadcasting were $34,050 in 2004. Broadcast news analysts had median earnings of $37,840.

Strategies for Finding the Jobs

Here are a few suggestions for starting your job search.

Get a Foot in the Door

In the world of newspapers, magazines, and book publishing, some experts suggest that you should take any available job so that you can get your foot in the door. For example, if you want to be an editor you could start out as a contract assistant, then move into an editorial position and up the ladder to senior editor or higher. If you get yourself in the door and get to know the people in the department where you hope to work, your chances are better than those of an unknown candidate wanting to advance immediately into an editorial position.

The same holds true for radio and television stations. Production assistants with a proven track record, for example, will move into higher level positions than job candidates off the street.

Prepare a Portfolio or Audition Tape

For photojournalists, a few different routes can be taken in the job-hunting process, but they all include putting together a professional portfolio. Some photojournalists identify the papers they would like to work for, and at their own expense they fly out on speculation to talk to the different editors—even when they know there are no current openings. This approach, although a bit costly for someone just starting out, can often work. The job applicant makes him- or herself known, and when an opening occurs, potential employers will remember your top-quality portfolio.

Job hunting through the mail can be just as effective. Send out your portfolio with a good cover letter, and don't be afraid to mention any story ideas you might have. Newspapers aren't looking for robots. They appreciate a photojournalist who does more than stand behind the camera and click the shutter. Follow up a week or so later as a reminder. You can make up your own picture postcards, using your best work. This helps jog the editor's memory—and shows your creativity.

Once they have a foot in the door, potential DJs and announcers should be ready to take any airtime slot offered, even if it's six o'clock on a Sunday morning. This gives you the opportunity to tape yourself. You can constantly update your tape and use it for auditions for more critical time slots.

Internships

Another successful method is to take more than the one required college internship. If you can get involved in two or even three internships, you'll make more contacts and increase your odds of lining up full-time employment when you graduate. At the same time, you'll be adding to your portfolio and creating impressive specifics to include on your résumé.

Related Occupations

Liberal arts majors acquire skills that can be transferred to a number of related occupations. Here is a representative list of the job titles in a few similar career paths; no doubt further investigation will reveal more.

Actor
Comedian

Documentary maker
Drama/music teacher
Educational film/video maker
Entertainer
Feature film director
Feature filmmaker
Feature film producer
Ghostwriter
Lyricist
Musician
Performing artist
Playwright
Poet
Visual artist

Help in Locating Employers

The following listings, directories, magazines, and resource books can help you in your job search. Most are available in the reference section of your library.

Broadcasting and Cable Yearbook
R.R. Bowker LLC
630 Central Ave.
New Providence, NJ 07974
bowker.com

Encyclopedia of Associations
Thomson Gale
gale.com

Gale Directory of Publications and Broadcast Media
Thomson Gale
gale.com

Guide to Literary Agents
Photographer's Market
Writer's Market
Writer's Digest Magazine
Writer's Digest Books

F & W Publications
1507 Dana Ave.
Cincinnati, OH 45207
writersdigest.com

The Literary Marketplace
Information Today, Inc.
143 Old Marlton Pike
Medford, NJ 08055
literarymarketplace.com

Professional Associations

Deciding which area of the media you would like to pursue and contacting a few of the related professional associations will help with your job search as well as your professional development. Professional associations offer conferences, seminars and workshops, a variety of publications, and job placement services.

Academy of Television Arts and Sciences
5220 Landershim Blvd.
North Hollywood, CA 91601-3109
emmys.org
Services: Educational programs and services, scholarship

The Accrediting Council on Education in Journalism and Mass Communications
University of Kansas School of Journalism
Stauffer-Flint Hall
1435 Jayhawk Blvd.
Lawrence, KS 66045-7575
www2.ku.edu/~acejmc
Services: List of schools with accredited programs in journalism, online newsletter

American Society of Journalists and Authors (ASJA)
1501 Broadway, Suite 302
New York, NY 10036
asja.org

Services: Publications, market search, conferences, information on contract negotiations, copyright, intellectual property, and similar issues

American Society of Magazine Editors
Magazine Publishers of America
810 Seventh Ave., 24th Floor
New York, NY 10019
magazine.org/editorial
Services: Seminar series, workshops, internships

American Society of Media Photographers
150 N. Second St.
Philadelphia, PA 19106
asmp.org
Services: Educational programs and seminars, publications

American Society of Newspaper Editors
11690B Sunrise Valley Dr.
Reston, VA 20191-1409
asne.org
Services: Convention, publications, grants for school newspapers

Association of American Publishers
50 F St., NW, Suite 400
Washington, DC 20001
publishers.org
Services: Seminars and workshops, book fairs, publications

Association of Authors' Representatives
aar-online.org
Services: Agent membership directory, newsletter

Association of Canadian Publishers
161 Eglinton Ave. E., Suite 702
Toronto, ON M4P 1J5
Canada
publishers.ca
Services: Conferences, book fairs, seminars, workshops

Association for International Broadcasting
PO Box 141

Cranbrook TN17 9AJ
United Kingdom
aib.org.uk
Services: Director of broadcasters, member forum

Broadcast Education Association
1771 N St.
Washington, DC 20036-2891
beaweb.org
Services: Training, educational materials, annual convention, publications, job placement

Canadian Association of Broadcasters
PO Box 627, Station B
Ottawa, ON K1P 5S2
Canada
cab-acr.ca
Services: Convention, awards, job listings

Canadian Association of Newspaper Editors
890 Yonge St., Suite 200
Toronto, ON M4W 3P4
Canada
cane.ca
Services: Seminars, awards

Canadian Association of Photographers and Illustrators in Communications
55 Mill St.
Case Goods Building 74, Suite 302
Toronto, ON M5A 3C4
capic.org
Services: Educational programs, networking

Canadian Community Newspapers Association
8 Market St., Suite 300
Toronto, ON M5E 1M6
Canada
ccna.ca
Services: Convention, publications, awards

Canadian Newspaper Association
890 Yonge St., Suite 200
Toronto, ON M4W 3P4
Canada
cna-acj.ca
Services: Career information, conferences, publications

Canadian Society of Magazine Editors
canadianeditors.com
Services: Awards, industry news

Dow Jones Newspaper Fund
4300 Route 1 N.
South Brunswick, NJ 08852
http://djnewspaperfund.dowjones.com/fund
Services: Information on careers in journalism, colleges and universities
offering degree programs in journalism or communications, and journalism
scholarships and internships

Magazines Canada
425 Adelaide St. W., Suite 700
Toronto, ON M5V 3C1
Canada
http://magazinescanada.ca
Services: Career information, newsletter, trade show

National Association of Broadcast Employees and Technicians
nabetcwa.org
Service: Career information

National Association of Broadcasters
1771 N St. NW
Washington, DC 20036
nab.org
Services: Publications, career information

National Association of Independent Publishers Representatives
111 East 14th St.
New York, NY 10003
naipr.org
Services: Publications, conferences, job listing

National Cable and Telecommunications Association
25 Massachusetts Ave. NW, Suite 100
Washington, DC 20001-1413
ncta.com
Services: Publications, career information

National Education Writers Association
2122 P St., NW Suite 201
Washington, DC 20037
ewa.org
Services: Publications, job bank, seminars, fellowships, contests

National Newspaper Association
PO Box 7540
Columbia, MO 65205-7540
nna.org
Services: Publications, career information

National Press Photographers Association
3200 Croasdaile Dr., Suite 306
Durham, NC 27705
nppa.org
Services: Workshops and seminars, self-training, competitions

Newspaper Association of America
4401 Wilson Blvd., Suite 900
Arlington, VA 22203-1867
naa.org
Services: Publications, conferences, seminars

The Newspaper Guild-CWA
501 Third St. NW
Washington, DC 20001-2797
newsguild.org
Services: Information on union issues for newspaper and magazine reporters

Radio-Television News Directors Association and Foundation
1600 K St. NW, Suite 700
Washington, DC 20006-2838
rtnda.org

Services: Publications, career information, job placement, scholarships, internships

Society for Technical Communication
901 North Stuart St., Suite 904
Arlington, VA 22203
stc.org
Services: Publications, competitions, grants, awards

Society of National Association Publications
8405 Greensboro Dr., #800
McLean, VA 22102
snaponline.org
Services: Seminars and resource networks, publications, job listings

Specialized Information Publishers Association
8201 Greensboro Dr., Suite 300
McLean, VA 22102
newsletters.org
Services: Career guide, awards, marketing tools

Writers Guild of America, East
555 West 57th St., Suite 1230
New York, NY 10019
wgaeast.org
Services: Union information, contests and competitions, fellowships and grants, workshops and conferences

Writers Guild of America, West
7000 West Third St.
Los Angeles, CA 90048
wga.org
Services: Union information, contests and competitions, fellowships and grants, workshops and conferences

Writers Guild of Canada
366 Adelaide St. West, Suite 401
Toronto, ON M5V 1R9
Canada
wgc.ca
Services: Union information for screenwriters, magazine, awards

9

Path 4: Advertising, Marketing, and Sales

We live in a world of choices. Just go into any supermarket in Canada or the United States and walk down the cereal or soap aisle. How many options line the shelves, whether for starting off the day or for washing clothes and dishes? Some would say too many, but that's not the point. In a free enterprise system, competition is the name of the game and to succeed, or just stay afloat, businesses have to attract the consumer with the biggest, tastiest, most colorful, most convenient, most healthful, or most efficient product or service.

Methods of reaching the consumer and getting a share of that dollar have permeated every aspect of our lives. One recent study determined that the average person is exposed to five thousand pieces of advertising each day. Advertising is all around us, through print and film, broadcasting and the Internet, and a host of other devices and campaigns. Consumers might sometimes see this bombardment as an intrusion; for liberal arts majors, it has opened the door to a wide range of employment possibilities.

Definition of the Career Path

Some of the careers explored in this chapter are indeed entered by graduates with field-specific majors (e.g., advertising majors go into advertising, marketing majors go into marketing). But graduates of liberal arts programs are blazing new trails as well as following well-established ones, through a variety of these areas. University communications departments now cover areas that were once the realms of different, separate departments. Communications departments offer programs that successfully compete with the departments of business, advertising, marketing, public relations, journalism, broadcasting, and other fields. To avoid missing out on potentially talented applicants, employers and human resources directors are becoming less strict in specifying particular majors when advertising open positions.

Here is a sample job advertisement within this career path that stresses skills and responsibilities rather than a major.

Account Executive. Expanding advertising agency seeks customer-service-oriented professional to provide strategic guidance and advertising expertise to a growing list of clients. Minimum requirements: bachelor's degree and three years' experience as a human resources generalist. Must have ability to establish and maintain long-standing relationships with major corporate clients, work independently, listen, and analyze client needs. Outgoing, poised individual with strong communication skills a must. Send résumé to . . .

Not only is a major not specified in the sample ad, but also the employer clearly seeks a generalist, someone who has not been pigeonholed by a work experience or university program. If you isolate the skills mentioned as requirements, you see that all could belong to a liberal arts major.

Advertising and Marketing Goals

Although advertising and marketing are distinct fields, they are often linked together. In simple terms, advertisers create a package to sell a product, service, or idea; marketing experts help select the audiences for the advertisement. The goal of advertising and marketing is to reach the consumer—to motivate or persuade a potential buyer; to sell a product, service, idea, or cause; to gain political support; or to influence public opinion. To aid in the advertising endeavor, marketing professionals poll public opinion or analyze the demographics and buying patterns of specific audiences. They play the role of researcher, statistician, social psychologist, and sociologist. With an idea of the specific audience to target, advertising professionals evaluate the competition, set goals and create a budget, design an advertisement—whether a simple three-line ad or a full-blown campaign—and determine what vehicle is best to reach that audience.

Most advertising agencies are organized into the following departments: agency management, account management, creative services, traffic control and production, media services, publicity and public relations, sales promotion, direct response, television production, and personnel. Agencies employ a number of professionals to perform a variety of duties in these departments.

Within smaller agencies, departments can be combined or services contracted out to independent subcontractors.

A FIRSTHAND ACCOUNT FROM TWO MARKETING PROFESSIONALS

Read the following accounts from two marketing specialists to learn what their work is really like.

Dennis Abelson, Marketing and Advertising Professional

Dennis Abelson is a founding partner of Matrix Partners, a marketing and communications firm. He has worked as a copywriter, associate creative director, and creative director. He has a B.A. in classical languages from Washington University in St. Louis, Missouri, and a M.S. in journalism and advertising from Northwestern University's Medill School of Journalism in Evanston, Illinois.

Getting Started

Dennis was a freelance writer who grew tired of the isolation and wanted to find some more lucrative creative challenges. Someone who had seen one of his promotional mailings for his writing approached him about starting a business, and together they began a full-service marketing, consulting, and communications firm. After a slow start, the company began to grow and become more successful. Dennis and his partner were able to disassociate themselves from a third partner and change the name of the company to Matrix Partners.

Matrix provides services that include packaging, advertising, promotion, direct mail, and sales presentations. Their diverse client roster includes a distributor of computer cabling and networking systems, an agricultural biotechnology company, a manufacturer of diving equipment, and several food vendors.

Typical duties for Dennis include revising and finalizing ad copy, attending project status meetings, reviewing logo designs for new accounts, performing online trademark searches for a proposed line, working with designers and writers, editing presentations, and meeting with clients. Although the hours are long, he enjoys the opportunity to be creative and to learn about many different industries, as well as the satisfaction of contributing to a client's success.

He also likes the fact that working in the creative end of advertising allows him to pursue his personal interests of audio engineering and cartooning.

continued

As an undergraduate, Dennis was program director for the campus radio station and creator of a weekly comic strip in the campus newspaper. Working in a creative field today adds to his enjoyment of his hobbies.

Advice from a Professional

Dennis has some succinct advice for others interested in this type of work. He says, "I would tell others who are considering a career in advertising and marketing to start with the largest organization that will hire you. And be prepared for the long haul."

Jane Ward, Senior Marketing Specialist

Jane Ward works as a marketing specialist for a software company. She has a bachelor of arts degree from Catholic University in Washington, D.C., where she majored in English with minors in French and philosophy, and a master of philosophy degree with a major in Irish literature from Trinity College in Dublin.

Getting Started

When Jane returned to the United States after earning her master's, she had difficulty finding a job, because she had very little work experience. She decided to learn Web publishing and soon found a job with a good salary. But she found the work boring and began to look for a more interesting position.

A job opened for a marketing specialist at a software company, and Jane knew that it was perfect for her. She had proven ability in learning the technical aspects of a job and provided some writing samples to the company. She was hired to create public relations and marketing materials, and she has since been promoted to senior marketing specialist.

Jane writes website content and manages the site by supervising the graphic designers and approving graphics for the site. She is responsible for press releases and ad copy, and she supervises the production of the company's ads. In addition, she attends several trade shows each year where she promotes the company to the press.

Jane enjoys her job, especially seeing something that she's written published in a magazine. She likes the relaxed work environment, which is common at software companies.

Advice from a Professional

Based on her experience, Jane offers some specific advice to aspiring marketing professionals. She says, "Learn how to look at the world around you with a critical eye. When an ad comes on television, pay attention to it. What was the goal of the people who created it? Who is the target market? What elements did they pull together to create the ad?

"Since I am involved in the writing end of marketing, I would recommend that you learn how to write truly well," she continues. "And I strongly recommend a liberal arts education, which teaches you how to think and how to articulate your thoughts. These are the kinds of tools that you need to achieve success in any industry."

Sales Goals

Each day, millions of dollars are spent on merchandise—everything from sweaters and cosmetics to lumber, office equipment, and plumbing supplies. Sales workers are employed by many retailers to assist customers in the selection and purchase of these items.

Whether selling antiques, computer equipment, or automobiles, a sales worker's primary job is to interest customers in the merchandise. This may be accomplished by describing the product's features, demonstrating its use, or showing various models and colors. For some jobs, particularly those selling expensive and complex items, special knowledge or skills are needed. For example, workers who sell home entertainment systems must be able to explain to customers the features of various brands and models, the meaning of manufacturers' specifications, and which components work best together.

The field of sales covers several different areas, including retail sales, from food to flowers; service sales, from hotel rooms to financial reporting systems; manufacturers' and wholesale sales, from books to computer disks; medical sales, from pharmaceuticals to hospital beds; travel sales; real estate sales; and insurance agents and brokers.

Possible Job Titles

A wide variety of job titles are available in this field, and many of those contain different rankings. For example, the position of account executive would have entry-level positions called assistant account executive or junior account executive; the next rank up would be associate account executive, moving on to senior account executive and account manager.

Account coordinator
Account director
Account/district manager

Account executive
Account specialist
Account supervisor
Account representative
Account trainee
Advertising director
Art buyer
Art director
Broadcast production manager
Consumer affairs specialist
Copyeditor
Copywriter
Creative director
Designer
Editor
Events coordinator
Graphic artist
Management supervisor
Market analyst
Market research manager
Media buyer
Media director
Media evaluator
Media placement specialist
Media planner
Media supervisor
Print production manager
Producer
Production assistant
Production manager
Project director
Promotion manager
Publicist
Research assistant
Researcher
Sales assistant
Sales planner
Sales representative
Spokesperson
Traffic assistant
Traffic manager

This list gives you an idea of the jobs available. You can add to the list as you investigate all the possibilities.

Possible Employers

Advertising and marketing professionals have the options to work in different settings, depending on their skills and interests.

Advertising Agencies

About one-third of advertising professionals work for ad agencies, which employ more than 500,000 throughout North America. A third are small, one-person offices; another third employ from two to five people; and the remaining third extend up to international megacompanies, such as Young & Rubicam, which has 168 agencies in eighty-one countries around the world.

New York continues to be the advertising hub of the world, with more than half of the top one hundred agencies headquartered there. But you don't have to move to New York to find work. As mentioned, many agencies have regional and international offices, and almost every major city, and even smaller ones, can claim their share of agencies.

Advertising agencies help clients—the advertisers—to identify potential customers, create effective advertisements, and arrange for the airtime or print space to run the advertising. Large agencies generally have a wide range of clients and can provide a new graduate with varied work experience. Starting your career off in a small agency, however, would allow you to quickly specialize in a particular area of advertising.

Marketing Firms/Departments

Marketers and advertising professionals work hand-in-hand, and thus many marketing departments are located within corporate advertising departments or in private advertising agencies. Private marketing firms function in a similar fashion to advertising agencies and work toward the same goals: identifying and targeting specific audiences that are receptive to specific products, services, or ideas.

Corporate Advertising Departments

Many corporations use the services of outside advertising agencies and marketing firms, just as many—especially the very large ones—operate their own in-house departments where workers create and develop the company's advertising and sales promotion material. For example, a large department store such as Macy's or Bloomingdale's has its professional staff create catalogs, brochures, newspaper inserts, flyers, and Internet advertising, as well as place the regular flow of daily newspaper ads. Developing this material is a big endeavor, requiring the skills of a variety of professionals, including copywriters, art directors, photographers, layout artists, and models.

Corporations that use the services of an outside agency might also maintain their own advertising department to function as a liaison between the agency and the company. In this case the staff is responsible for ensuring that the advertising being produced meets the company's objectives and is placed in the appropriate media outlets.

Self-Employed/Freelancers

Freelance "ad men" hire their services to advertising agencies and corporations. They are usually consulted when staffing is not sufficient to handle a new client or there is a sudden overload of work. Freelancers are also successful when working with small businesses that don't have the desire or budget to work with a large, expensive agency.

They can pick and choose their projects, although that is usually not an option when just starting out. Once established, a freelancer with enough clients can open his or her own office. As the client load increases, so does the need to have help. This is how many small agencies get their start: an enterprising freelancer builds up enough business to take on employees.

Freelance publicists work with people who, simply put, need publicity. For example, a former politician wants to get on the university campus speaker circuit, or perhaps an independent film company with a small-time budget wants a chance at big-time distribution.

Publishing Companies

Large publishing companies, especially those located in New York City, operate publicity departments to promote their authors and books. Some of the duties of a publicist working in this setting include arranging for point-of-sale material (e.g., printed bookmarks) to be made available at bookstores; organizing book tours, including scheduling speaking engagements on television and radio shows as well as setting up book-signing engagements; and writing jacket copy.

Bookstores

More and more bookstores, especially the new superstores, coordinate events designed to attract customers. A publicist is needed who can book local authors for speaking and signing engagements, arrange for cookbook authors to give cooking demonstrations, and find other ways to appeal to the tastes of the book-buying public.

Vacation Resorts/Chambers of Commerce

Promoting a vacation spot or city is another option for publicists. Publicists working for a vacation resort would produce pamphlets, brochures, press releases, and perhaps video demonstrations and websites of the location's selling points. Their target audience would be travel agents, travel writers and editors, and the vacationing public. Publicists working for chambers of commerce direct their efforts at potential businesses and new residents as well as vacationers and other visitors.

Other settings include but are not limited to the following:

- Retail stores
- Manufacturing companies
- Wholesale firms
- Medical supply houses
- Travel agencies
- Insurance firms
- Real estate brokerage houses

Working Conditions

In this competitive business, every industry is vying for the all-important consumer dollar. The working atmosphere might be challenging and exciting, but also hectic and stressful.

For example, a busy ad agency has a long list of ongoing projects needing attention at the same time. No matter how large the agency is or how many professionals it employs, the workload often strains available staff. This atmosphere lends itself to employees feeling overworked, and burnout can be common after a few years of constant pressure.

To attract clients and beat the competition, agencies work hard to develop campaigns and present their concepts to clients. The account managers must accurately determine the client's goals, or the campaign will be off target and the agency may lose the account. Even when a campaign is successful, pressure still exists to keep the client by continuing to provide excellent service.

Working hours can be long and disruptive to personal life. The work can also include a good deal of travel to meet with clients or attend conferences. Although to many outsiders the life of an advertising executive might seem glamorous, in reality the work is less secure than most, with staff layoffs occurring when the workload drops.

Training and Qualifications

The good news for liberal arts majors is that for most entry-level professional and managerial positions in advertising and public relations, a bachelor's degree with a broad liberal arts exposure is preferred.

Which liberal arts major you choose may be determined by the area you intend to pursue in this career path. If you are aiming for the title of account manager, courses in marketing, business and finance, and speech communications are as important as advertising theory. Potential art directors obviously need technical training in drawing, illustration, and graphic design. If you want to work in sales for a highly specialized product such as pharmaceuticals or electronics, you might want to pursue additional courses in that area. All are well-served, however, by courses in effective communications.

To work in advertising, you should have good people skills, common sense, creativity, communication skills, and problem-solving ability. Foreign language skills have always been important for those wanting to work abroad for domestic firms or to represent foreign firms domestically. However, these skills are increasingly vital to reach linguistic minorities in U.S. cities such as Los Angeles, New York, Miami, Houston, and Phoenix. New media, such as the Internet, are creating opportunities to market products, but also are increasing the need for additional training for those already employed. Keeping pace with technology is fundamental to success in the industry. In addition, advertisers must keep in tune with the changing values, cultures, and fashions of society.

Career Outlook

Competition for many advertising jobs will be keen because the excitement of the industry traditionally attracts many more job seekers than there are job openings. Employment in the industry is projected to grow 22 percent through 2014, compared with 14 percent for all industries combined. New jobs will be created as the economy expands and generates more products and services to advertise. Increased demand for advertising and marketing services also will stem from growth in the number and types of media outlets used to reach consumers, creating opportunities for people skilled in preparing material for presentation on the Internet.

In addition to new jobs created, job openings will arise as workers transfer to other industries or leave the workforce. On the other hand, employment growth may be tempered by the increase of efficient nonprint media advertising, such as Internet or radio, which could replace some workers. Employment also may be adversely affected if legislation aimed at protecting public health and safety further restricts advertising for specific products such as alcoholic beverages and tobacco. Layoffs are common in advertising and public relations services firms when accounts are lost, major clients cut budgets, or agencies merge.

Positions such as advertising, marketing, promotions, public relations, or sales manager are highly coveted and will be sought by other managers or highly experienced professionals, resulting in keen competition. College graduates with related experience, a high level of creativity, and strong communication skills should have the best job opportunities. In particular, employers will seek those who have the computer skills to conduct advertising, marketing, promotions, public relations, and sales activities on the Internet.

Employment of these managers is expected to increase between 18 and 26 percent through 2014, spurred by intense domestic and global competition in products and services offered to consumers. However, projected employment growth varies by industry. For example, employment is projected to grow much faster than average in scientific, professional, and related services (e.g., such as computer systems design or advertising), as businesses increasingly hire contractors for these services instead of additional full-time staff. By contrast, a decline in employment is expected in many manufacturing industries.

Earnings

Median annual earnings in 2004 were $63,610 for advertising and promotions managers, $87,640 for marketing managers, and $84,220 for sales managers.

Median earnings in the industries employing the largest numbers of marketing managers were as follows:

Computer systems design and related services	$107,030
Management of companies and enterprises	$98,700
Insurance carriers	$86,810
Architectural, engineering, and related services	$83,610

Median annual earnings in the industries employing the largest numbers of sales managers in 2004 were as follows:

Computer systems design and related services	$119,140
Wholesale electronic markets, agents, and brokers	$101,930
Automobile dealers	$97,460
Management of companies and enterprises	$95,410
Machinery, equipment, and supplies merchant wholesalers	$84,680

Salary levels vary substantially, depending on the level of managerial responsibility, length of service, education, size of firm, location, and industry. For example, manufacturing firms usually pay these managers higher salaries than do nonmanufacturing firms. For sales managers, the size of their sales territory is another important determinant of salary. Many managers earn bonuses equal to 10 percent or more of their salaries.

Strategies for Finding the Jobs

As in the corporate world, you should become a familiar fixture in an advertising agency's reception area. Sending out blind résumés has never been an effective method for finding a job in any profession. Have a good portfolio with you, one that showcases your best work. Then, you'll be able to quickly open and display it if the right person takes interest. If you are interested in copywriting, visuals are less important than writing samples and a good marketing sense. Aspiring art directors need samples of their work that show their design ability.

Persistence is a valued trait in this career path; showing the same quality in your job search can help pay off. The strategies mentioned in Chapter 6 also apply here. Use your university's resources as well as those available at the library. Here are some additional tips:

- Start your job search before you near graduation. Arranging an internship will give you an edge, because you will have already become a familiar face on the job. When an opening occurs, a known commodity (who performed well during the internship) is going to be chosen over an unknown one.
- Learn as much as you can about the agency or firm you're interested in. In other words, target your prospects.

Related Occupations

The skills liberal arts majors use in advertising, marketing, sales, publicity, and promotion can also be transferred to different settings. For example, a market analyst who is adept at collecting and interpreting data on different populations could also work for the government as a demographer helping to prepare a census, or with an insurance company as an actuarian.

Actuarian
Advertising photography
Campaign developer
Convention sales
Demographer
Function-sales manager
Fund-raiser
Hotel sales
Membership-services director
Researcher
Statistician
Travel photography

Help in Locating Employers

The following list includes contacts, journals, and directories that can aid in your job search. Many of the publications are available as reference material at local libraries.

Advertising Age
Crain Communications, Inc.
711 Third Ave.
New York, NY 10017-4036
adage.com

Adweek
adweek.com

Brandweek
770 Broadway

New York, NY 10003
brandweek.com

Encyclopedia of Associations
Thomson Gale
gale.com

Mediaweek
770 Broadway, 7th Floor
New York, NY 10003
mediaweek.com

Standard Directory of Advertisers (The Advertiser Red Book)
Standard Directory of Advertising Agencies (The Agency Red Book)
National Register Publishing
890 Mountain Ave, 3rd Floor
New Providence, NJ 07974
nationalregisterpub.com

   The Agency Red Book lists more than four thousand agencies and includes regional offices, accounts specializations, number of employees, and names and titles of key personnel. It is published every February, June, and October.

Professional Associations

The following list of professional associations gives you an idea of the variety of professional associations available within this career path. It only takes a letter or a phone call to receive detailed information about an association and the professional area it supports.

The Advertising Club of New York
theadvertisingclub.org
Services: Annual advertising and marketing course with classes in copywriting, special graphics, verbal communication, advertising production, and others; publications; membership directory; Young Professionals group

Ad Council
1203 19th St. NW, 4th Floor
Washington DC, 20036

adcouncil.org
Services: Conducts public service advertising campaigns, publications

Advertising Photographers of America, Inc. (APA)
PO Box 250
White Plains, NY 10605
apanational.com
Services: Lectures, seminars, discussion groups, publications

Advertising Research Foundation
432 Park Ave. S.
New York, NY 10016
thearf.org
Services: Annual meeting, regional meetings, workshops, conferences, publications

Advertising Women of New York
25 West 45th St., Suite 403
New York, NY 10036
Services: Annual career conference for college seniors, publications, job listings

American Advertising Federation
Education Services Department
1101 Vermont Ave. NW, Suite 500
Washington, DC 20005-6306
aaf.org
Services: Training, internships, conferences, awards, competitions

American Association of Advertising Agencies
405 Lexington Ave., 18th Floor
New York, NY 10174-1801
aaaa.org
Services: Job locating, conferences, training

American Marketing Association
311 South Wacker Dr., Suite 5800
Chicago, IL 60606
marketingpower.org
Services: Seminars, conferences, student marketing clubs, placement service, publications

Association of National Advertisers
708 Third Ave.
New York, NY 10017-4270
ana.net
Services: Conducts studies, surveys, seminars, and workshops; provides a specialized education program; publishes the Advertiser

Canadian Advertising Research Foundation
160 Bloor St. E., Suite 1005
Toronto, ON M4W 1B9
Canada
carf.ca
Services: Nonprofit research organization, seminars and workshops, speaker series, newsletter

Canadian Marketing Association
1 Concorde Gate, Suite 607
Don Mills, ON M3C 3N6
Canada
the-cma.org
Services: Offers courses in marketing techniques, student programs, certification

Canadian Professional Sales Association
310 Front St. W., Suite 800
Toronto, ON M5V 3B5
Canada
Services: Training, certification, newsletter, career center

National Council for Marketing and Public Relations
PO Box 333069
Greeley, CO 80633
ncmpr.org
Services: Annual conference, national surveys, needs assessment, awards, publications

Point of Purchase Advertising International
popai.com
Services: Conducts student education programs, publications

Retail Advertising & Marketing Association
325 7th St., NW, Suite 1100
Washington, DC 20004-2802
rama-nrf.org
Services: Conducts annual conference, offers education programs for retail marketers

Sales and Marketing Executives International
PO Box 1390
Sumas, WA 98295-1390
smei.org
Services: Job listings, conferences, training, publications, business services

10

Path 5: The Helping Professions

Awide variety of occupations can be included in the helping professions career path. Positions ranging from clinical psychologist or social worker to rehabilitation or vocational counselor fit in this category. For some jobs, a B.A. in psychology or a related liberal arts field is sufficient; for others, a master's or doctoral degree is required.

While helping professionals might come to their fields with a variety of backgrounds and training, they usually have a few traits and skills in common. The ability to listen and empathize, a tolerance of and sensitivity to individuals who may be different from themselves, and a sincere desire to help without judging are all qualities they must share.

Definition of the Career Path

The job titles listed in this section all fall within the helping professions. However, this list is by no means exhaustive. During your job search, you can use it as a reference, adding to it as you come across notices for jobs that mention related skills.

Each job title requires different levels of training and education, and each has a different set of working conditions and job settings. However, some have a great deal of overlap in duties and responsibilities. A counselor working in a mental health clinic might function the same way a therapist would working in a private practice. After the list, you will find a more detailed description of three of the major occupational categories in the helping professions: human services workers, mental health and rehabilitation counselors, and psychologists.

Academic counselor
Alcohol counselor
Case management aide
Career counselor
Child abuse worker
Child psychiatrist
Child psychologist
Clinical psychologist
Clinical social worker
Community outreach worker
Drug abuse counselor
Educational counselor
Educational therapist
Gerontology aide
Guidance counselor
Marriage and family counselor/therapist
Mental health counselor
Mental health technician
Psychiatric nurse
Psychiatrist
Psychologist
Psychotherapist
Rehabilitation counselor
Residential counselor
Social service technician
Social work assistant
Social worker
Special education teacher
Spiritual counselor
Substance abuse counselor
Therapist
Vocational counselor

Human Services Workers

Human services worker is a generic term for those with various job titles, such as alcohol counselor, case management aide, child abuse worker, community outreach worker, drug abuse counselor, gerontology aide, mental health technician, residential counselor, social service technician, and social work assistant.

Human services workers generally work under the supervision of social workers or, in some cases, psychologists. The level of responsibility and supervision they are given varies depending on the job; some work on their own most of the time and have little direct supervision, while others work under close direction.

Human services workers assist clients in obtaining benefits or services. They assess the client's need for and eligibility to receive services by examining financial documents, such as rent receipts and tax returns. The workers determine whether the client is eligible for food stamps, Medicaid, or other welfare programs and also inform clients on how to access services; arrange for transportation and escorts, if necessary; and provide emotional support. Human services workers monitor and keep case records on clients and report progress to supervisors.

Responsibilities often include transporting or accompanying clients to group meal sites, adult day-care programs, or doctors' offices; calling or visiting clients' homes to make sure services are being received; or helping to resolve disagreements, such as those between tenants and landlords.

These professionals also take on roles in community settings, such as organizing and leading group activities, assisting clients in need of counseling or crisis intervention, or administering a food bank or emergency fuel program. Some work in halfway houses and group homes and oversee the adult residents who need some supervision or support on a daily basis. They review clients' records, and confer with families and medical personnel to gain better insight into the clients' background and needs. To promote independence, they may teach residents to prepare their own meals and to do other housekeeping activities. The professionals also provide emotional support and lead recreation activities.

In psychiatric hospitals and psychiatric clinics, these workers may help clients master everyday living skills and teach them how to communicate more effectively and get along better with others. They often assist with music, art, and dance therapy and with individual and group counseling and lead recreational activities.

Depending on the setting, working conditions generally vary. Many spend part of their time in an office or group residential facility, and the rest in the field visiting clients or taking them on trips or meeting with people who provide services to the clients. Most work a regular forty-hour week, although some evening and weekend work may be necessary. Residential settings usually require shift work because residents need around-the-clock supervision.

While satisfying, the work can be emotionally draining, with understaffing and lack of equipment adding to the pressure. Turnover is reported to be high, especially among workers without academic preparation for this field.

Training and Qualifications

While a few employers hire high school graduates, you will need at least some college preparation in human services, social work, one of the social or behavioral sciences, or another related liberal arts degree to qualify for most jobs in the helping professions. A four-year degree is your best bet for staying ahead of the competition. The level of formal education you have generally influences the kind of work you will be assigned and the amount of responsibility entrusted to you. If you enter this field with no more than a high school education, you will most likely perform clerical duties; if you have a college degree, you are more likely to be assigned to do direct counseling, coordinate program activities, or manage a group home.

Employers may also look for experience in other occupations or leadership experience in school or in a youth group, so courses in social work, psychology, sociology, rehabilitation, or special education are particularly helpful. Most employers provide in-service training such as seminars and workshops.

You'll need appropriate personal qualifications to serve people who are vulnerable to exploitation or mistreatment, since many clients come from unstable surroundings. In addition to the relevant academic preparation, any volunteer or work experience will serve you well. Patience, understanding, and a strong desire to help others are highly valued characteristics. Other important personal traits include communication skills, a strong sense of responsibility, and the ability to manage time effectively. Hiring requirements in group homes tend to be more stringent than in other settings.

More than four hundred certificate- and associate-degree programs in human services or mental health are offered at community and junior colleges, vocational-technical institutes, and other postsecondary institutions throughout the United States and Canada. About the same number of programs offer a bachelor's degree in human services, and a small number of programs lead to a master's degree in human services administration.

Most academic programs in this field will prepare you for specialized roles in human services. You will be exposed early and often to the kinds of situations you may encounter on the job. Programs typically include courses in psychology, sociology, crisis intervention, social work, family dynamics, therapeutic interviewing, rehabilitation, and gerontology. Through classroom simulation internships, you will learn interview, observation, and record-keeping skills; individual and group counseling techniques; and program planning.

A formal education is most certainly required to advance in this field. In group homes, completion of a one-year certificate in human services along with several years of experience may suffice for promotion to supervisor. However, in general, advancement requires a bachelor's or master's degree in counseling, rehabilitation, social work, or a related field.

Career Outlook

Overall employment in the field of social service are expected to be excellent through 2014. Job prospects will vary depending on location and specialization, so opportunities generally should be very promising because the number of job openings that arise should exceed the number of graduates in this field. There will be more competition for jobs in urban areas than in rural areas, but qualified applicants should have little difficulty finding employment. Confronted with rapid growth in the demand for social and human services, many employers increasingly rely on social and human service assistants to undertake greater responsibility for delivering services to clients.

Opportunities are expected to be good in private social service agencies, which provide such services as adult day care and meal delivery programs. Employment in private agencies will grow as state, provisional, and local governments continue to contract out services to the private sector in an effort to cut costs. With a growing elderly population, demand for social services will expand. In addition, more social and human service providers and assistants are required to provide services to pregnant teenagers, the homeless, the mentally disabled and developmentally challenged, and substance abusers. Some private agencies have been employing more social and human service assistants in place of social workers, who are more educated and, thus, more highly paid.

Job training programs also are expected to require additional workers in social and human services. As social welfare policies shift focus from benefit-based programs to work-based initiatives there will be more demand for people to teach job skills to the people who are new to, or returning to, the workforce.

Residential care establishments should face increased pressures to respond to the needs of the mentally and physically disabled. Many of these patients have been deinstitutionalized and lack the knowledge or the ability to care for themselves. Also, more community-based programs and supportive independent-living sites are expected to be established to house and assist the homeless and the mentally and physically disabled. As substance abusers are increasingly being sent to treatment programs instead of prison, employment of social and human service assistants in substance abuse treatment programs also will grow.

Earnings

Median annual earnings of social and human service assistants were $24,270 in 2004. The majority earned between $19,220 and $30,900, while the top 10 percent earned more than $39,620, and the lowest 10 percent earned less than $15,480.

Median earnings in the industries employing the largest numbers of these workers were:

State government	$29,270
Local government	$28,230
Individual and family services	$23,400
Vocational rehabilitation services	$21,770
Residential mental retardation, mental health, and substance abuse facilities	$20,410

A FIRSTHAND ACCOUNT FROM A HUMAN SERVICES WORKER

Read the following personal account to learn about the work of a human services professional who specializes in residential counseling.

M. Allen Broyles, Residential Counselor

M. Allen Broyles has worked for fifteen years in a group home for people who are mentally impaired, where he is responsible for teaching independent-living skills to the residents. Jadwin House is owned by Sunderland Family Treatment Services, an outpatient counseling service organization for the community. It houses up to eight residents who have been released from mental institutions and want to learn how to live on their own.

Allen teaches the residents independent-living skills, including such tasks as personal hygiene, money management, time management, and cooking skills—basically, all the skills and tools each individual may need to live on his or her own. He works the swing shift, from 3:00 P.M. to 11:00 P.M., which is the busiest shift of the day. At the beginning of each shift, Allen is briefed by the day shift about any unusual developments, such as new residents, new procedures, or medicine changes. By this time of day many residents are gone, with some at another facility that offers training in working skills, some at doctor's appointments, and others tending to their own routines.

Allen makes any necessary changes in medications and procedures. He checks to see which resident is assigned cooking duty, and together they prepare the evening meal. All items on the menu are brought from the food storage area, and the resident is brought up to speed on what is going to be prepared. The resident decides what he or she will do in preparation. Allen offers instruction on how to accomplish the tasks, and he performs the remainder of the cooking to finish the meal. He strives to make the evening meal a pleasant experience, especially since the residents have so few pleasures in their lives. To achieve this, the resident cook sets the table and serves the meal home style, which allows the residents to interact with each other at mealtime. After dinner, the cook cleans the kitchen, and other residents are assigned cleaning chores, which Allen oversees.

At 8:00 P.M., Allen monitors the residents' evening medications. After this is done, the residents settle into their evening routines such as watching TV, listening to the stereo, or going out for walks. The house is usually quiet from 9:00 P.M. to 11:00 P.M., which is when Allen works on paperwork or his own personal writing. He often watches television with the residents. When his relief arrives at 11:00 P.M., Allen briefs him on the house activities and any developments before going home.

The Up- and Downsides of the Profession

Allen enjoys being able to help people with their second, third, or even fourth chances in life, and he has had the satisfaction of witnessing some dramatic turnarounds. He recalls a resident named Harry who arrived disheveled and haggard-looking. His schizophrenia made him so delusional that the staff could not communicate with him, and paranoia gripped him so tightly that he was afraid to leave the home. Over the three years that Harry stayed at Jadwin House, he improved steadily until he was able to move to his own apartment.

A resident named Joanie was so affected by paranoia that she left her room only for meals. Allen and the rest of the staff thought she might have to return to the hospital, but over time she learned to control her problems and now lives on her own and holds a steady job.

The only downside that Allen mentions is the hopeless feeling he experiences when a resident has to be readmitted to the hospital.

Advice from a Professional

"First and foremost, you must be the type of person who interacts well with others," Allen advises. "Do you want to have an impact on people's lives—sometimes at great cost? Are you willing to put up with all the downsides of mental illness to see the positive effects later? Do you really care about the well-being of those less fortunate than yourself?

"Second, you must educate yourself as much as possible. The higher your education and the more specialized that education is, the more successful you will find yourself within your chosen field."

Mental Health and Rehabilitation Counselors

Counselors assist people with personal, family, social, educational, and career decisions, problems, and concerns. Their duties depend on the individuals they serve and the settings in which they work.

Mental Health Counselors

Mental health counselors emphasize prevention. They work with individuals and groups to promote optimum mental health and help individuals cope with addictions and substance abuse; family, parenting, and marital problems; suicide; stress management; problems with self-esteem; issues associated with aging; job and career concerns; educational decisions; and issues of mental and emotional health. Mental health counselors work closely with other specialists, including psychiatrists, psychologists, clinical social workers, psychiatric nurses, and school counselors.

Some counselors specialize in a particular social issue or population group, such as marriage and family, grief counseling, multicultural, and gerontological counseling. A gerontological counselor may provide services to elderly people who face changing lifestyles because of health problems, as well as help families cope with these changes. A multicultural counselor might help employers adjust to an increasingly diverse workforce.

Rehabilitation Counselors

These professionals help people deal with the personal, social, and vocational impacts of their disabilities. They evaluate clients' strengths and limitations; provide personal and vocational counseling; and may arrange for medical care, vocational training, and job placement. Rehabilitation counselors interview people with disabilities and their families; evaluate school and medical reports; and consult and plan with physicians, psychologists, occupational therapists, employers, and others. In consultation with the client, they develop and implement a rehabilitation program, which may include training to help foster independence and employability. They also work toward increasing the client's capacity to adjust and live independently.

Counselors work in a wide variety of public and private settings, including health-care facilities; vocational rehabilitation centers; social agencies; correctional institutions; and residential care facilities, such as halfway houses for criminal offenders and group homes for children, the aged, and the disabled. They also work in organizations engaged in community improvement and social change, as well as drug and alcohol rehabilitation programs and state and local government agencies. A growing number of counselors work in health maintenance organizations (HMOs), insurance companies, group practice, and private practice, spurred by laws allowing counselors to receive payments from insurance companies, and requiring employers to provide rehabilitation services to injured workers.

Self-employed counselors and those working in mental health and community agencies, often work evenings to counsel clients who work during the day. Rehabilitation counselors generally work a standard forty-hour week.

Training and Qualifications

You will need a master's degree in mental health counseling, counseling psychology, gerontological counseling, marriage and family counseling, substance abuse counseling, rehabilitation counseling, agency or community counseling, or a related field to work in this area. Most graduate-level counselor education programs in colleges and universities are in departments of education or psychology. Courses are grouped into eight core areas:

- Human growth and development
- Social and cultural foundations
- Helping relationships
- Groups
- Lifestyle and career development
- Appraisal
- Research and evaluation
- Professional orientation

An accredited program includes forty-eight to sixty semester hours of graduate study, including a period of supervised clinical experience in counseling. The Council for Accreditation of Counseling and Related Educational Programs (CACREP) accredits graduate counseling programs in counselor education and in community, gerontological, mental health, school, student affairs, and marriage and family counseling. In 2007, 203 programs were accredited in the United States and Canada.

Many counselors choose to be certified by the National Board for Certified Counselors (NBCC), which grants the general practice credential of National Certified Counselor. To meet the NBCC requirements, you must hold a master's degree in counseling, have at least two years of professional counseling experience, and pass the National Counselor Examination. National certification is voluntary and distinct from state certification. However, in some states, those who pass the national exam are exempt from taking a state certification exam. NBCC also offers specialty certification in career, gerontological, school, and clinical mental health counseling.

To work as a mental health counselor you will need a master's degree in mental health counseling, another area of counseling, or in psychology or social work. You may become voluntarily certified by the National Board of Certified Clinical Mental Health Counselors. Generally, to receive this certification as a mental health counselor, you will need to have a master's degree in counseling, two years of post-master's experience, a period of supervised clinical experience, a taped sample of clinical work, and a passing grade on a written examination.

Generally, vocational and related rehabilitation agencies require a master's degree in rehabilitation counseling, counseling and guidance, or counseling psychology for rehabilitation counselor jobs. However, in some situations you may be accepted with a bachelor's degree in rehabilitation services, counseling, psychology, or related fields. A bachelor's degree in counseling will qualifies you to work as a counseling aide, rehabilitation aide, or social service worker. Experience in employment counseling, job development, psychology, education, or social work may be helpful.

The Council on Rehabilitation Education (CORE) accredits graduate programs in rehabilitation counseling. A minimum of two years of study including a period of supervised clinical experience are required for the master's degree. Some colleges and universities offer a bachelor's degree in rehabilitation services education. In most state vocational rehabilitation agencies, applicants must pass a written examination and be evaluated by a board of examiners. Many employers require rehabilitation counselors to be certified. To become certified by the Commission on Rehabilitation Counselor Certification, counselors must graduate from an accredited educational program, complete an internship, and pass a written examination. They are then designated as Certified Rehabilitation Counselors.

Some employers provide training for newly hired counselors. Many have work-study programs so that employed counselors can earn graduate degrees. Counselors must participate in graduate studies, workshops, institutes, and personal studies to maintain their certificates and licenses.

If you are interested in working in counseling, you should have a strong interest in helping others and the ability to inspire respect, trust, and confidence. You should also be able to work independently or as part of a team.

Career Outlook

For counselors, prospects should be excellent in rehabilitation, substance abuse, and behavioral disorder counseling.

Employment of school counselors is expected to grow with increases in student enrollments at postsecondary schools and colleges and as more jurisdictions require elementary schools to employ counselors. The responsibilities of school counselors are expanding, which should also lead to increases in their employment. For example, counselors are becoming more involved in crisis and preventive counseling, helping students deal with issues ranging from drug and alcohol abuse to death and suicide.

Demand for vocational or career counselors should grow as multiple job and career changes become common for workers and as workers become increasingly aware of the counselors' services. In addition, many governments will employ growing numbers of counselors to assist beneficiaries of welfare programs who exhaust their eligibility and must find jobs. Other opportunities for employment counselors will arise in private job-training centers that provide training and other services to laid-off workers and others seeking to acquire new skills or new careers.

The demand for substance abuse and behavioral disorder counselors is expected to be strong because drug offenders are increasingly being sent to treatment programs rather than to jail. The statewide networks that are being established to improve services for children and adolescents with serious emotional disturbances and for their family members will need to be staffed with mental health counselors. Under managed-care systems, insurance companies are increasingly providing for reimbursement of counselors as a less costly alternative to psychiatrists and psychologists.

The numbers who will need rehabilitation counseling are expected to grow as advances in medical technology allow more people to survive injury or illness and live independently again. In addition, legislation requiring equal employment rights for people with disabilities will spur demand for counselors, who not only help these people make a transition into the workforce but also help companies to comply with the law.

Employment of mental health counselors and marriage and family therapists will grow as more individuals become comfortable with seeking professional help for a variety of health, personal, and family problems. Employers are also increasingly offering employee assistance programs that provide mental health and alcohol and drug abuse counseling. More people are expected to use these services as society focuses on ways of developing mental well-being, such as controlling stress associated with job and family responsibilities.

Earnings

Median annual earnings of educational, vocational, and school counselors in 2004 were $45,570. Most earned between $34,530 and $58,400. The lowest 10 percent earned less than $26,260, and the highest 10 percent earned more than $72,390. School counselors can earn additional income working summers in the school system or in other jobs. Median annual earnings in the industries employing the largest numbers of these counselors were as follows:

Elementary and secondary schools	$51,160
Junior colleges	$45,730
Colleges, universities, and professional schools	$39,110
Individual and family services	$30,240
Vocational rehabilitation services	$27,800

Median annual earnings of counselors in other areas were as follows:

Substance abuse and behavioral disorder counselors	$32,130
Mental health counselors	$32,960
Rehabilitation counselors	$27,870
Marriage and family therapists	$38,980

For substance abuse, mental health, and rehabilitation counselors, government employers generally pay the highest wages, followed by hospitals and social service agencies. Residential care facilities often pay the lowest wages.

Self-employed counselors who have well-established practices, as well as counselors employed in group practices, usually have the highest earnings.

Psychologists

Psychologists study the human mind and behavior to understand, explain, and change people's behavior. Those who work in research investigate the physical, cognitive, emotional, or social aspects of human behavior. Psychologists in health-service provider fields provide mental health care in hospitals, clinics, schools, or private settings. Psychologists employed in applied settings, such as business, industry, government, or nonprofits, provide training, conduct research, design systems, and act as advocates for psychology.

Like other social scientists, psychologists formulate hypotheses and collect data to test their validity. The research methods they use vary depending on the topic under study, and may include gathering information through controlled laboratory experiments or by administering personality, performance, aptitude, or intelligence tests. Additional methods include observation, interviews, questionnaires, clinical studies, and surveys.

Psychologists apply their knowledge to a wide range of endeavors, including health and human services, management, education, law, and sports.

In addition to working in a variety of settings, psychologists usually specialize in one of a number of different areas.

Clinical Psychologists

The members of this largest specialty of psychology mostly work in counseling centers, independent or group practices, hospitals, or clinics. They help mentally and emotionally disturbed clients adjust to life and may assist medical and surgical patients in dealing with illnesses or injuries. Some work in physical rehabilitation settings, treating patients with spinal cord injuries, chronic pain or illness, stroke, arthritis, and neurological conditions. Others help people deal with times of personal crisis, such as divorce or the death of a loved one.

Clinical psychologists often interview patients and administer diagnostic tests. They provide individual, family, or group psychotherapy and may design and implement behavior modification programs. Some collaborate with physicians and other specialists to develop and implement treatment and intervention programs that patients can understand and comply with. Others work in universities and medical schools, where they train graduate students in the delivery of mental health and behavioral medicine services. Some administer community mental health programs.

Clinical psychology includes three major areas of specialization. First, health psychologists design and administer health maintenance counseling programs meant to help people achieve particular goals, such as weight loss or smoking cessation. Second, neuropsychologists study the relation between the brain and behavior. To gain this understanding, they often work in stroke and head injury programs. Third, geropsychologists deal with the special problems that the elderly face. The emergence and growth of these specialties reflects the increasing participation of psychologists in providing direct services to special patient populations.

Counseling Psychologists

Using various techniques, including interviewing and testing, these psychologists advise people on how to deal with problems of everyday living. They work in settings such as university counseling centers, hospitals, and individual or group practices.

Developmental Psychologists

These professionals study the physiological, cognitive, and social development that occurs throughout life. They may also study developmental disabilities and their effects. Some specialize in behavior during infancy, childhood, and adolescence, or changes that occur during maturity or old age. In the latter case, research is developing ways to help elderly people remain independent as long as possible.

Experimental or Research Psychologists

This group works in university and private research centers and in business, nonprofit, and governmental organizations. They study the behavior of human beings and that of animals such as rats, monkeys, and pigeons that might offer clues to human behaviors. Prominent areas of study in experimental research include motivation, thought, attention, learning and memory, sensory and perceptual processes, effects of substance abuse, and genetic and neurological factors affecting behavior.

Industrial and Organizational Psychologists

In the interest of improving productivity and the quality of work life, industrial and organizational psychologists apply psychological principles and research methods to the workplace. They are also involved in research on management and marketing problems. Their methods include screening, training, and counseling job applicants, as well as performing organizational development and analysis. Industrial psychologists might work with management to reorganize the work setting to improve productivity or quality of life in the workplace. They frequently act as consultants, brought in by management to solve a particular problem.

School Psychologists

These professionals are employed in elementary and secondary schools, where they collaborate with teachers, parents, and school personnel to create safe, healthy, and supportive learning environments for all students. Their responsibilities include addressing students' learning and behavior problems; improving classroom management strategies or parenting skills; countering substance abuse; assessing students with learning disabilities and gifted and talented students to help determine the best way to educate them; and improving teaching, learning, and socialization strategies. They also may evaluate the effectiveness of academic programs, prevention programs, behavior management procedures, and other services provided in the school setting.

Cognitive Psychologists

Some cognitive psychologists are involved with research related to computer programming and artificial intelligence.

Social Psychologists

They work in organizational consultation, marketing research, systems design, or other applied psychology fields, examining people's interactions with others and with the social environment. Prominent areas of study include group behavior, leadership, attitudes, and perception.

Other Psychology Specialists

Other areas of specialization in psychology include psychometrics, psychology and the arts, history of psychology, psychopharmacology, and community, comparative, consumer, engineering, environmental, family, forensic, population, military, and rehabilitation psychology.

In addition to the jobs described, many are employed as psychology faculty at colleges and universities and as high school psychology teachers.

Working Conditions

The subfield or job setting will determine a psychologist's working condition. For example, clinical, school, and counseling psychologists in private practice have their own offices and set their own hours, but they often offer evening and weekend hours to accommodate their clients. Those employed in hospitals, nursing homes, and other health-care facilities may work shifts that include evenings and weekends, while those who work in schools and clinics generally work regular hours.

Psychologists employed as college and university faculty members divide their time between teaching and research. The may also have administrative responsibilities, and many also have part-time consulting practices. Most psychologists in government and industry have structured schedules.

Increasingly, many psychologists are working as part of a team, consulting with other psychologists and professionals. Many experience pressures because of deadlines, tight schedules, overtime, and frequently disrupted schedules. Travel may be required in order to attend conferences or conduct research.

Training and Qualifications

If upon entering the field you have a bachelor's degree in psychology, you will be qualified to assist psychologists and other professionals in community mental health centers, vocational rehabilitation offices, and correctional programs. Additional job possibilities include working as a research or administrative assistant for psychologists, or working as a technician in a related field such as marketing research. Some graduates with bachelor's degrees in psychology work in other areas such as sales or business management.

In the U.S. federal government, candidates who have at least twenty-four semester hours in psychology and one course in statistics qualify for entry-level positions. However, you should expect strong competition for these jobs because this is one of the few areas in which you can work as a psychologist without an advanced degree.

To build a career in psychology, you'll definitely need a graduate degree. Once you've earned a master's degree, you will be qualified to work as an industrial-organizational psychologist. You may also work as a psychological assistant under the supervision of doctoral-level psychologists and may conduct research or psychological evaluations. You'll have to devote at least two years of full-time graduate study to earn a master's degree in psychology, including practical experience in an applied setting and a master's thesis based on an original research project.

A doctoral degree is needed to work as an independent licensed clinical or counseling psychologist. As a psychologist, a Ph.D. is qualified for a wide range of teaching, research, clinical, and counseling positions in universities, health-care services, elementary and secondary schools, private industry, and government. Someone with a doctor of psychology (Psy.D.) degree may work in clinical positions or in private practices but also may teach, conduct research, or carry out administrative responsibilities.

A doctoral degree generally requires five to seven years of graduate study, culminating in a dissertation based on original research. As an integral part of your program, you will study quantitative research methods, including the use of computer-based analysis. The Psy.D. may be based on practical work and examinations rather than a dissertation. In clinical or counseling psychology, the requirements for the doctoral degree include at least a one-year internship.

In most states, you would be required to have a specialist degree to work as a school psychologist, although a few still credential school psychologists with master's degrees. A specialist (Ed.S.) degree in school psychology requires a minimum of three years of full-time graduate study (at least sixty graduate semester hours) and a one-year internship. Because their professional practice addresses educational and mental health components of students' development, school psychologists' training includes coursework in both education and psychology. All Canadian provinces except the Yukon Territory have licensing requirements for school psychologists.

You should expect keen competition for admission to graduate psychology programs. Some universities require you to have an undergraduate major in psychology, while others prefer only coursework in basic psychology with courses in the biological, physical, and social sciences and in statistics and mathematics.

The American Psychological Association (APA) accredits programs in the United States and Canada, including doctoral training programs in clinical, counseling, and school psychology, as well as accrediting institutions that provide internships for doctoral students in school, clinical, and counseling psychology. With the assistance of the National Council for Accreditation of Teacher Education, the Canadian Psychological Association and the National Association of School Psychologists are also involved in the accreditation of advanced degree programs in school psychology.

Psychologists in independent practice or those who offer any type of patient care, including clinical, counseling, and school psychologists, must meet certification or licensing requirements in all provinces, states and the District of Columbia. Licensing laws vary by jurisdiction and by type of position and require licensed or certified psychologists to limit their practice to areas in which they have developed professional competence through training and experience. Clinical and counseling psychologists usually require a doctorate in psychology, the completion of an approved internship, and one to two years of professional experience in addition to passing a standardized examination. Some states and provinces require continuing education for renewal of the license.

The National Association of School Psychologists (NASP) awards the Nationally Certified School Psychologist (NCSP) designation, which recognizes professional competency in school psychology at a national, rather than state, level. Currently, twenty-six states recognize the NCSP and allow those with the certification to transfer credentials from one state to another without taking a new certification exam. Requirements for the NCSP include the completion of sixty graduate semester hours in school psychology; a 1,200-hour internship, 600 hours of which must be completed in a school setting; and a passing score on the National School Psychology Examination.

The American Board of Professional Psychology (ABPP) acknowledges professional achievement to practitioners in the United States and Canada by awarding specialty certification, primarily in clinical psychology, clinical neuropsychology, and counseling, forensic, industrial-organizational, and school psychology. Candidates for ABPP certification need a doctorate in psychology, postdoctoral training in their specialty, five years of experience, professional endorsements, and a passing grade on an examination.

Aspiring psychologists interested in direct patient care must be emotionally stable, mature, and able to deal effectively with people. Sensitivity, compassion, good communication skills, and the ability to lead and inspire others are particularly important qualities for those wishing to do clinical work and counseling. Research psychologists should be able to perform work both independently and as part of a team. Patience and perseverance are vital qualities, because achieving results in the psychological treatment of patients or in research may take a long time.

Career Outlook

Employment of psychologists is expected to grow between 18 and 26 percent through 2014, based on growing demand for psychological services in schools, hospitals, social service agencies, mental health centers, substance abuse treatment clinics, consulting firms, and private companies.

Among the specialties in this field, the best job opportunities are expected to be for school psychologists, especially those with a specialist degree or higher. Growing awareness of how students' mental health and behavioral problems affect learning is increasing demand for school psychologists to offer student counseling and mental health services.

Clinical and counseling psychologists will be needed to help people cope with depression and other mental disorders, marriage and family problems, job stress, and addiction. Health-care costs associated with unhealthy lifestyles, such as smoking, alcoholism, and obesity, are rising and prevention and treatment are more critical. An increase in the number of employee assistance programs that help workers deal with personal problems should also spur job growth in clinical and counseling specialties.

Industrial-organizational psychologists will be needed to help to boost worker productivity and retention rates in a wide range of businesses. They will be needed to help companies deal with issues such as workplace diversity and antidiscrimination policies. Companies also will use psychologists' expertise in survey design, analysis, and research to develop tools for marketing evaluation and statistical analysis.

Demand should be particularly strong for graduates with doctorates from leading universities in applied specialties such as counseling, health, and school psychology. Psychologists with extensive training in quantitative research methods and computer science may have a competitive edge over applicants without that background.

For those with master's degrees in fields other than industrial-organizational psychology, competition should be stiff because of the limited number of positions that require only a master's degree. Master's degree holders may find jobs as psychological assistants or counselors, providing mental health services under the direct supervision of a licensed psychologist. Still others may find jobs involving research and data collection and analysis in universities, government, or private companies.

Opportunities directly related to psychology will be limited for bachelor's degree holders. Some may find jobs as assistants in rehabilitation centers or in other jobs involving data collection and analysis. Those who meet state or provincial certification requirements may become high school psychology teachers.

Earnings

Median annual earnings of salaried clinical, counseling, and school psychologists in 2004 were $54,950. Most earned between $41,850 and $71,880, while the lowest 10 percent earned less than $32,280, and the highest 10 percent earned more than $92,250.

Median earnings in the industries employing the largest numbers of these psychologists were:

Offices of other health practitioners	$64,460
Elementary and secondary schools	$58,360
Outpatient care centers	$46,850
Individual and family services	$42,640

Median annual earnings of salaried industrial-organizational psychologists in 2004 were $71,400, with most earning between $56,880 and $93,210. The lowest 10 percent earned less than $45,620, and the highest 10 percent earned more than $125,560.

Salaries of psychologists in Canada vary by occupation and geographic area. Service Canada reports that in 2004, psychologists working in Saskatchewan had the highest hourly income of $36.92. The lowest rate was found in Nova Scotia, where hourly earnings ranged from $19.80 to $34.15.

Strategies for Finding the Jobs

For any of the helping professions, there are some tried-and-true strategies to secure a job in your chosen field. The following steps are offered by clinical psychologist Dr. Gerald Oster.

Mentors

Talk to your professors: they are there as models and as valuable resources, and they want to help. Let them know your interests and career goals. Based on their years of experience, they have valuable contacts and can steer you in the right direction.

A FIRSTHAND ACCOUNT FROM A MENTAL HEALTH PROFESSIONAL

A clinical psychologist has shared an account of his work. Read on to learn more about this profession.

Gerald D. Oster, Ph.D., Clinical Psychologist

Dr. Gerald D. Oster is a licensed psychologist with a private practice in Maryland, where he specializes in individual and family therapy. He is a former clinical associate professor of psychiatry at the University of Maryland School of Medicine in Baltimore. In more than twenty years of practice, he has worked in state hospitals, outpatient clinics, and residential treatment centers.

Dr. Oster earned his B.A. in sociology at the University of South Florida, Tampa; his M.A. in psychology at Middle Tennessee State University in Murfreesboro; and his Ph.D. in psychology at Virginia Commonwealth University in Richmond.

Working at more than one job led to a great deal of variety. Dr. Oster spends Monday working in his private practice. On Tuesday mornings, he spends two hours at a community mental health center in Baltimore's inner city, where he works as a child and family therapist. He describes two patients he is working with: one is a sixteen-year old boy who has served time in juvenile delinquent centers and is trying to reenter the community, while struggling to fit in at school and in his foster home; the other is a kindergarten-age boy who lives with his grandparents in a dangerous neighborhood and is very insecure about his environment. In addition to working with these patients, Dr. Oster handles a tremendous amount of paperwork that is required by the various governing agencies that monitor the clinic.

After his morning at the clinic, he spends eight hours at the University Counseling Center, working with students who have come to the center for help in coping with issues such as school stress, relationship problems, and caring for dependents. Following this, he usually goes to his private practice to catch up on work or see a patient in the evening.

The other days are similar but involve different demands and different settings. Dr. Oster is often at the local community hospital interviewing or administering tests to a suicidal patient or out-of-control adolescent. His private practice is divided between seeing children and adults with various kinds of troubles.

Although he is quite busy, he has to seek out new ways to maintain his practice, especially in the context of the managed care system. This has become the case for many psychologists in solo private practice, who must handle confusing paperwork and payment reimbursement problems that can affect the services they offer to their patients.

Getting Started

Dr. Oster began his undergraduate studies as a business major, but found his courses in sociology much more interesting. He enjoyed studying topics such as social and political theory and how people adapt to environmental and economic changes. He also found that learning about and helping people in all aspects of life filled a personal need to go beyond his own boundaries and provide support to people in stress.

It was not until several years after receiving his undergraduate degree (and owning a bookstore) that he could focus his thoughts into a single direction. Dr. Oster believes that this waiting period is fairly common among college graduates, since few students have a specific career direction in view and go through college with the hope that their degree will get them a specific job. It can take several years to make a career choice and turn toward something that you love and want to pursue full-time.

For Gerald Oster, psychology was that path. At first he wanted to be a criminal psychologist and found courses in personality and psychopathology fascinating. He also enjoyed courses in child development with a talented professor who could demonstrate the early cognitive and emotional stages of life. This led to his pursuit of a master's degree. For a time, he worked in the juvenile justice system, providing evaluations for the courts on delinquents. However, through the support of his professors and his own continuing interest in other aspects of psychology, he entered a doctoral program that provided exposure to a greater depth and breadth of psychology.

While studying for his doctorate, he worked in a rat laboratory, was part of a developing center for aging, taught courses in developmental psychology and child development, and was exposed to continuing clinical work through practicums at child development centers and psychiatric units for the aged. He also participated with many research teams on topics of learning theory, intellectual testing, and cognitive changes over the life span.

Dr. Oster's professional career began at a private research firm that subcontracted work from the National Institutes of Health, where he was involved with coordinating research projects for a nationwide study on depression. After one year, he decided to return to clinical work and took a job in a state hospital as a psychologist on an adolescent unit. During that time, he also consulted for a geriatric unit and continued his learning through weekly seminars and clinical rounds.

Several years later, after having obtained his independent professional license, Dr. Oster changed locations and jobs. He began working at a residential treatment center for emotionally disturbed children and adolescents, where he later became director of psychology internship training. He continued his own training, which included studies in family therapy, and he became interested in expanding his private practice and pursuing the writing he had begun during this time. With this in mind, he resigned from the treatment center and took on a series of part-time positions.

Dr. Oster has coauthored six professional books on psychological testing and therapy. He has also cowritten a trade book, *Helping Your Depressed Teenager: A Guide for Parents and Caregivers*. His most recent book is *Life as a Psychologist: Career Choices and Insights*.

Advice from a Professional

Based on his extensive experience as a psychologist, Dr. Oster offers this advice: "'Learning is a lifelong process. Degrees only give you permission to learn.' These were words from an uncle and ring true in today's world. Most people anticipate change, and you can expect to change career paths several times during a lifetime. Thus, going to college and possibly to graduate school allows you the exposure to valuable technical skills and other social, intellectual, and educational possibilities."

Attend Professional Conventions

Participate in seminars and to conventions. You'll find no better place to see the possibilities a profession offers than at a national convention. You will gain incredible exposure and an awareness of what the field is all about.

Build up Your Résumé

Becoming an assistant—whether it is in teaching or research, or within your college's counseling center—is an excellent way to discover what your strengths and weaknesses are. You can decide if could see yourself doing this work on a daily basis. Take as many practicums or internships as possible. And if your schedule allows, work full-time or volunteer during the summers.

Related Occupations

Here are descriptions of related areas in the helping professions in which liberal arts majors can find work.

Human Services Workers
Workers in other occupations that require skills similar to those of human services workers include social workers, community outreach workers, religious workers, occupational therapy assistants, physical therapy assistants and aides, psychiatric aides, and activity leaders.

Mental Health Counselors
Counselors help individuals determine their interests, abilities, and disabilities, and deal with personal, social, academic, and career problems. Others who help people in similar ways include college and student personnel workers, teachers, personnel workers and managers, human services workers, social workers, psychologists, psychiatrists, clergy, occupational therapists, training and employee development specialists, and equal employment opportunity and affirmative action specialists.

Psychologists
Psychologists are trained to conduct research and teach, evaluate, counsel, and advise individuals and groups with special needs. Others who do this kind of work include psychiatrists, social workers, sociologists, clergy, special education teachers, and counselors.

Professional Associations

Contact the following associations for further information on the various helping professions.

Human Services Workers
Council for Standards in Human Service Education
PMB 703
Larrabee Ave., Suite 104
Bellingham, WA 98225-7367
cshse.org

National Organization for Human Services
5601 Brodie Ln., Suite 620-215

Austin, TX 78745
nationalhumanservices.org

Counselors

American Counseling Association
5999 Stevenson Ave.
Alexandria, VA 22304
Canada
counseling.org

Canadian Counselling Association
16 Concourse Gate, Suite 600
Ottawa, ON K2E 7S8
Canada
ccacc.ca

Council for Accreditation of Counseling and Related Educational Programs
American Counseling Association
5999 Stevenson Ave.
Alexandria, VA 22304
cacrep.org

Commission on Rehabilitation Counselor Certification
300 North Martingale Rd., Suite 460
Schaumburg, IL 60173
crccertification.org

National Board for Certified Counselors
3 Terrace Way
Greensboro, NC 27403
nbcc.org

State and provincial departments of education can supply information on colleges and universities that offer approved guidance and counseling training for state certification and licensure requirements.

State and provincial employment service offices have information about job opportunities and entrance requirements for counselors.

Psychologists
American Psychological Association
750 First St. NE
Washington, DC 20002-4242
apa.org

Canadian Psychological Association
141 Laurier Ave. W., Suite 702
Ottawa, ON K1P 5J3
Canada
cpa.ca

Canadian Association of School Psychologists
10660 Trepassey Dr.
Richmond, BC V7E 4K7
Canada
cpa.ca/CASP

National Association of School Psychologists
4030 East West Hwy., Suite 402
Bethesda, MD 20814
nasponline.org

Information about state licensing requirements is available from the following:

Association of State and Provincial Psychology Boards
PO Box 241245
Montgomery, AL 36124-1245
asppb.org

Information on obtaining a job with the U.S. federal government may be obtained from the website usajobs.com, which lists all available federal positions. For federal jobs in Canada, visit jobs-emplois.gc.ca.

11

Path 6: Law

Many students use their liberal arts bachelor's degree as a stepping-stone to careers that require additional education and training. The options for professional careers beyond the bachelor's level seem almost limitless. Many are discussed in other chapters as well as in the introductory sections to this book. But this chapter focuses on law, a wide-open field for which a liberal arts B.A. is the best preparatory background.

Preparation for a career as a lawyer begins in college. Although there is no specific prelaw major, the choice of an undergraduate program is an important foundation for future law studies. Certain courses and activities are preferable because they provide the skills needed to succeed both in law school and in the profession.

The essential skills include proficiency in writing, reading, analyzing, thinking logically, and communicating verbally. The best choice is an undergraduate program that cultivates these skills while broadening your view of the world. Courses in English, a foreign language, public speaking, government, philosophy, history, economics, mathematics, and computer science are useful. Whatever the major, you should not specialize too narrowly, but instead attempt to gain the broadest possible educational background.

If you are interested in a particular aspect of law, you may find related courses helpful. For example, many law schools with patent-law tracks require a bachelor's degree, or at least several courses, in engineering and science. Future tax lawyers should have a strong undergraduate background in accounting.

Definition of the Career Path

Attorneys, or lawyers, operate in our culture as both advocates and advisors. As advocates, they represent one of the opposing parties in criminal and civil trials by presenting evidence that supports their client in court. As advisors, they counsel their clients as to their legal rights and obligations and suggest particular courses of action in business and personal matters. In either role, all attorneys use their research and communication skills to interpret the law and apply it to specific situations. Research skills are used to conduct in-depth investigations into the purposes behind the applicable laws and into judicial decisions that have been applied to those laws under circumstances similar to those currently faced by the client.

All lawyers continue to make use of law libraries to prepare cases, but most supplement their research with Internet searches and computer software packages that automatically search the legal literature and identify legal texts that may be relevant to a specific subject. They also use computers to organize and index their material in cases that involve many supporting documents. Lawyers also use electronic filing, videoconferencing, and voice-recognition technology to share information more effectively with other parties involved in a case. After completing their research, attorneys make recommendations as to what actions they may take in a specific case. They also draw up legal documents, such as wills and contracts.

Lawyers must deal with people in a courteous, efficient manner and must maintain strict confidentiality, not disclosing matters discussed with clients. They hold positions of great responsibility and are obligated to adhere to strict rules of ethics.

Possible Job Titles

While most lawyers work in private practice where they may concentrate on criminal or civil law, an attorney can enter into many specialized areas.

Trial Lawyers
The specifics of a lawyer's job depend on the area of specialization and position. Even though all lawyers are allowed to represent parties in court, some appear in court more frequently than others, and some specialize in trial work. These lawyers must have an exceptional ability to think quickly and speak with ease and authority and need to be thoroughly familiar with courtroom rules and strategy. Trial lawyers still spend most of their time outside the

courtroom conducting research, interviewing clients and witnesses, and handling other details in preparation for trial.

Criminal Law

Lawyers who specialize in criminal law represent people who have been charged with crimes and argue their cases in courts of law. Some work as public defenders, representing people charged with criminal acts who are unable to afford the services of a private attorney.

Civil Law

In civil law, attorneys assist clients with litigation, wills, trusts, contracts, mortgages, titles, and leases. Some manage a person's property as trustee or, as executor, see that provisions of a client's will are carried out. Others handle only public interest cases, civil or criminal, that have a potential impact extending well beyond the individual client.

Other lawyers work for legal-aid societies private, nonprofit organizations established to serve disadvantaged people. These lawyers generally handle civil rather than criminal cases.

Some other specializations within civil law include the following:

- Bankruptcy
- Probate
- International law
- Environmental law
- Intellectual property
- Insurance law
- Family law
- Real estate law
- Public defense

House Counsel

Some lawyers are employed full-time by a single client. If the client is a corporation, the lawyer is known as house counsel and usually advises the company about legal questions that arise from its business activities. These questions might involve patents, government regulations, contracts with other companies, property interests, or collective-bargaining agreements with unions.

Government Attorneys

Attorneys are employed at the various levels of government. Lawyers who work for state attorneys general, prosecutors, public defenders, and courts play a key role in the criminal justice system. At the federal level, attorneys investigate cases for the Department of Justice or other agencies. Also, lawyers at every government level help develop programs, draft laws, interpret legislation, establish enforcement procedures, and argue civil and criminal cases on behalf of the government.

Law Clerks

Law clerks, also called research attorneys, work with a particular judge, either for a one- to two-year stint out of law school or as a full-time, professional career. Their duties vary depending on the judge they work with, but in general, reading briefs, writing notes on them, and conducting research are a law clerk's main responsibilities.

Law Professors

A relatively small number of trained attorneys work in law schools. Most are faculty members who specialize in one or more subjects, and others serve as administrators. Some work full-time in nonacademic settings and teach only part-time.

Working Conditions

Lawyers work primarily in offices, law libraries, and courtrooms. They occasionally meet in clients' homes or places of business and, when necessary, in hospitals or prisons. They frequently travel in order to attend meetings; to gather evidence; and to appear before courts, legislative bodies, and other authorities.

Salaried lawyers employed by government and private corporations generally have structured work schedules. Those in private practice may work irregular hours while conducting research, conferring with clients, or preparing briefs during nonoffice hours. Lawyers often work long hours, and about half regularly work fifty hours or more per week. They are under particularly heavy pressure, for example, when a case is being tried, because preparation for court includes keeping abreast of the latest laws and judicial decisions.

Although work generally is not seasonal, the work of tax lawyers and other specialists may be an exception. Because lawyers in private practice can often determine their own workload and when they will retire, many stay in practice well beyond the usual retirement age.

A FIRSTHAND ACCOUNT FROM A COURT OFFICIAL

Read the following personal account to learn about the work of an attorney employed in a court system.

Gist Fleshman, Clerk of the Court

Gist Fleshman is clerk of the court for the Appellate Court of Illinois, Third District. He has a bachelor's degree in political science from Illinois State University in Normal, Illinois. After working for a congressman in Washington, D.C., for a couple of years, he returned to school and earned his J.D. from DePaul University in Chicago.

The clerk of the court is the head administrative official in a court, the person who runs the court's daily operations. Gist's official job title is Clerk of the Appellate Court/Attorney, which distinguishes him from clerks of the court who are not attorneys. Illinois has clerks of the court at the trial level (circuit court) who are elected officials. Those in the appellate and state supreme courts are appointed clerks.

Gist says that his job is about 40 percent legal and 60 percent administrative. As the day-to-day operations manager for the court, he deals with the public and press in addition to handling all the motions filed in the court. Since the court receives thousands of motions, the judge has authorized Gist and some other staff members to handle most of the work. When an issue is particularly complex, Gist confers with a motions judge.

In his administrative capacity, Gist makes sure that the staff members do their jobs. He makes some policy decisions and is responsible for building maintenance. He also supervises eighteen employees, including staff attorneys, the chief deputy clerk and seven deputy clerks, and the maintenance and housekeeping staff. The court's six judges each have two law clerks and one secretary.

Gist says that his job offers variety without stress, unlike some other legal settings. He has the opportunity to do legal work and the freedom to decide how much of it he wants to do. He can delegate tasks to the research department or conduct his own research on an issue he finds particularly interesting.

The downside for Gist is handling personnel problems, which is common in administrative positions. He has found that the best approach is to handle a problem directly and to discuss it privately with the employee involved.

continued

One of the things he loves about the job is the ability to make a differ-ence. Gist says, "You definitely see injustices, where people have gotten a bad deal—people in prison who shouldn't be, or children who were taken away needlessly from their parents. Unlike in other jobs, you can do some-thing about it here. You can pick up the phone and talk to a judge and tell him what's going on. You often become an advocate for a particular party. Nevertheless, the judges listen to me. Wrongs can be righted. I love that aspect. It's very gratifying."

Getting Started
Gist earned his undergraduate degree in political science. He enjoyed the field, but didn't want to do that work for his entire career. He took some time off and realized that he needed more than a political science degree, something that would allow him to enter into a job immediately. He decided to pursue a degree in law.

He originally planned to practice law, but came to the Third District Appel-late Court directly out of law school as a staff attorney. The court had a cen-tral research staff that functions the way law clerks do. Gist thought he'd stay for one or two years and then enter private practice. After a year he went to a few interviews and was offered some jobs, but they didn't interest him. Since he enjoyed his job, he decided to stay another year, and eventually two judges asked him if he'd like to be their personal law clerk, a position that came with a $7,000 raise.

Again, he thought he would do this for a year and then move on, but when the research director resigned, Gist was offered that position. He was now the day-to-day supervisor of the central staff attorneys, a position that he held for over two years until he was named Clerk of the Court. Gist has been with the court for over fifteen years, longer than any of the judges.

Advice from a Professional
Based on his many years of experience in the legal profession, Gist offers some advice to anyone interested in a career in the courts. "You need to work your way up through the ranks," he says. "The courts want someone with experience. Coming in as a staff attorney or law clerk is the best way to do it because you learn how the court works.

"In some ways it's a position you can create for yourself. If you prove yourself, you could make the job whatever you want it to be."

"It's a very competitive field. You need to make sure you have excellent reading and writing skills."

Training and Qualifications

The United States and Canada have different requirements for the practice of law.

U.S. Requirements

To practice law in the courts of any state or other jurisdiction, an attorney must be licensed, or admitted to its bar, under rules established by the jurisdiction's highest court. All states require applicants for admission to the bar pass a written examination; most states also require applicants to pass a separate written ethics examination. In some cases, lawyers who have been admitted to the bar in one state may be admitted to the bar in another without taking an examination if they meet the latter jurisdiction's standards of good moral character and a specified period of legal experience. In most cases, however, lawyers must pass the bar examination in each state in which they plan to practice. Federal courts and agencies set their own qualifications for those practicing before or in them.

To qualify for the bar examination in most states, you will need a college degree and must graduate from a law school accredited by the American Bar Association (ABA) or the proper state authorities. ABA accreditation signifies that the law school, particularly its library and faculty, meets certain standards developed to promote quality legal education. As of 2005, there were 191 ABA-accredited law schools; others were approved by state authorities only. With certain exceptions, graduates of schools not approved by the ABA are restricted to taking the bar exam and practicing in the state or other jurisdiction in which the school is located; most of these schools are in California. In 2005, seven States (California, Maine, New York, Vermont, Virginia, Washington, and Wyoming) accepted the study of law in a law office as qualification for taking the bar examination; three jurisdictions (California, the District of Columbia, and New Mexico) now accept the study of law by correspondence. Several states require registration and approval of students by the state Board of Law Examiners, either before the students enter law school or during their early years of legal study.

Although no nationwide bar examination exits, forty-eight states, the District of Columbia, Guam, the Northern Mariana Islands, Puerto Rico, and the Virgin Islands require the six-hour Multistate Bar Examination (MBE) as part of the overall bar exam; the MBE is not required in Louisiana or Washington. The MBE covers a broad range of issues, and sometimes a locally prepared state bar examination is given in addition to it. The three-hour Multistate Essay Examination (MEE) is used as part of the bar exam in several states. States vary in their use of MBE and MEE scores.

Many states also require Multistate Performance Testing (MPT) to assess the practical skills of beginning lawyers. Requirements vary by state, although the test is usually taken at the same time as the bar exam and is a one-time requirement.

The required college and law school education typically takes seven years of full-time study after high school, consisting of four years of undergraduate study, followed by three years of law school. You must have a bachelor's degree to qualify for admission to law school. To meet the needs of students who can attend only part-time, a number of law schools have night or part-time divisions, which usually require four years of study; about one in ten graduates from ABA-approved schools attended part-time.

Acceptance by most law schools will depend on your ability to demonstrate an aptitude for the study of law, usually through good undergraduate grades, the Law School Admission Test (LSAT), the quality of the undergraduate school you attended, any prior work experience, and sometimes, a personal interview. However, law schools vary in the weight they place on each of these and other factors.

You must take the LSAT to apply to any law school approved by the ABA. Most schools also require that you have certified transcripts sent to the Law School Data Assembly Service, which then submits your LSAT scores and the standardized records of your college grades to the law schools of your choice. Both this service and the LSAT are administered by the Law School Admission Council. You should be prepared for intense competition for admission to many law schools, especially the most prestigious ones, with the number of applicants greatly exceeding the number that can be admitted.

During the first year of law school you will take core courses such as constitutional law, contracts, property law, torts, civil procedure, and legal writing. In the remaining time, you may elect specialized courses in specific fields such as tax, labor, or corporate law. Law students often acquire practical experience by participating in school-sponsored legal clinic activities; in the school's moot court competitions, in which students conduct appellate arguments; in practice trials under the supervision of experienced lawyers and judges; and through research and writing on legal issues for the school's law journal.

A number of law schools have clinical programs where students gain legal experience through practice trials and projects under the supervision of practicing lawyers and law school faculty. For example, law school clinical programs might include work in legal aid clinics, or on the staff of legislative committees. Part-time or summer clerkships in law firms, government agencies, and corporate legal departments also provide valuable experience. Such training can lead directly to a job after graduation and can help you to decide what kind of practice best suits you. Clerkships also may be an important source of financial aid.

In 2004, law school graduates in fifty-two jurisdictions were required to pass the Multistate Professional Responsibility Examination (MPRE), which tests their knowledge of the ABA codes on professional responsibility and judicial conduct. In some states, the MPRE may be taken during law school, usually after completing a course on legal ethics.

Law school graduates receive the degree of juris doctor (J.D.) as the first professional degree. An advanced law degree may be desirable if you plan to specialize, research, or teach. You may also pursue a joint degree program, which usually requires an additional semester or year of study. Joint degree programs are offered in a number of areas, including law and business administration or public administration.

Canadian Requirements

The legal profession in Canada is a self-governing body, regulated in each province by a law society that determines whether an applicant can be licensed to practice law. The basic procedure for a prospective lawyer is to graduate from an approved law school and complete the bar admission course in the province in which you want to practice.

The academic prerequisite for taking the bar admission course is either graduation from a common law program approved by the law society, in a university in Canada, or a certificate of qualification issued by the National Committee on Accreditation. Sixteen universities in Canada offer law courses approved by the law society; you must meet the requirements of the specific university in order to study law. An approved law course takes three years to complete and leads to a bachelor of laws (LL.B.) or doctor of jurisprudence (J.D.) degree.

The specific requirements for the bar admission course differ among the provinces, but in general the course comprises three phases: a skills phase, a substantive/procedural phase, and an articling phase. The skills and substantive/procedural phases usually run from eight to ten weeks each. The articling phase (i.e., the development of practical legal skills under the supervision of a lawyer) can last ten to twelve months. The bar examination is taken upon successful completion of the bar admission course. All lawyers must join the Law Society in the province where they practice.

General Information

A great deal of responsibility is involved in the practice of law. In planning your law career, you should like to work with people and be able to win the respect and confidence of clients, associates, and the public. Perseverance, creativity, and reasoning ability also are essential to lawyers, who often analyze complex cases and handle new and unique legal problems.

Like most attorneys, you will likely start your career in a salaried position, probably working as a research assistant to experienced lawyers or judges. After several years of salaried employment with progressively more responsibility, you may be admitted to partnership in a firm or go into private practice. After years of practice, some lawyers become full-time law school faculty or administrators; a growing number have advanced degrees in other fields as well.

Some use their legal training for administrative or managerial positions in various departments of large corporations. A transfer from a corporation's legal department to another department often is viewed as a way to gain administrative experience and rise in the ranks of management.

Regardless of your career path, stay informed about legal and nonlegal developments that affect your practice. Currently, forty states and jurisdictions mandate continuing legal education (CLE). Many law schools, state and local bar associations, and provincial law societies provide continuing education courses that help lawyers stay abreast of recent developments. Some jurisdictions allow CLE credits to be obtained through participation in Internet seminars.

Career Outlook

Lawyers across North America hold more than 800,000 jobs. Approximately three out of four practice privately, either as partners in law firms or in solo practices. Most salaried lawyers work in government or with corporations or nonprofit organizations. Many salaried lawyers working outside of government are employed as house counsel by public utilities, banks, insurance companies, real estate agencies, manufacturing firms, and other business firms and nonprofit organizations. Some also have part-time independent practices, while others work part-time as lawyers and full-time in another occupation.

Employment of lawyers is expected to grow between 9 and 17 percent through 2014, primarily as a result of growth in the population and in the general level of business activities. Job growth among lawyers also will result from increasing demand for legal services in such areas as health care, intellectual property, venture capital, energy, elder, antitrust, and environmental law. In addition, the wider availability and affordability of legal clinics should result in increased use of legal services by middle-income people.

However, as businesses attempt to cut costs by using large accounting firms and paralegals to perform some of the functions handled by attorneys, demand for lawyers will become limited. For example, accounting firms may provide employee-benefit counseling, process documents, or handle various other services previously performed by a law firm. Also, mediation and dispute resolution increasingly are being used as alternatives to litigation.

Given the large number of students who graduate from law schools each year, competition for job openings should continue to be strong, with the best opportunities occurring for graduates with superior academic records from highly regarded law schools. Perhaps as a result of competition for attorney positions, lawyers are increasingly finding work in nontraditional areas for which legal training is an asset, but not normally a requirement, such as administrative, managerial, and business positions in banks, insurance firms, real estate companies, government agencies, and other organizations. Employment opportunities are expected to continue to arise in these organizations at a growing rate.

As in the past, some graduates may have to accept positions in areas outside of their field of interest or for which they feel overqualified. Some recent law school graduates who have been unable to find permanent positions are turning to the growing number of temporary staffing firms that place attorneys in short-term jobs until they are able to secure full-time positions. This service allows companies to hire lawyers on an "as-needed" basis and permits beginning lawyers to develop practical skills while looking for permanent positions.

Because of the stiff competition for jobs, a law graduate's work experience and willingness to relocate assume greater importance. However, relocation may require taking an additional state bar examination in order to be licensed to practice in a different location. In addition, employers are increasingly seeking graduates who have advanced law degrees and experience in a specialty, such as tax, patent, or admiralty law.

Employment growth for lawyers will continue to be concentrated in salaried jobs, as businesses and all levels of government employ a growing number of staff attorneys and as employment in the legal services industry grows. Most salaried positions are in urban areas where government agencies, law firms, and big corporations are concentrated.

The number of self-employed lawyers is expected to decrease slowly, reflecting the difficulty of establishing a profitable new practice in the face of competition from larger, established law firms. The growing complexity of law, which encourages specialization, along with the cost of maintaining up-to-date legal research materials, also favors larger firms.

For attorneys who wish to work independently, establishing a new practice will probably be easiest in small towns and expanding suburban areas, where there is likely to be less competition from larger firms. New lawyers may also find it easier to become known to potential clients in smaller settings.

Some lawyers are adversely affected by cyclical swings in the economy. For example, during recessions fewer clients request discretionary legal services such as planning estates, drafting wills, and handling real estate transactions. Also, corporations are less likely to litigate cases when declining sales and profits result in budgetary restrictions. Some corporations and law firms will not hire new attorneys until business improves, and these establishments may even cut staff to contain costs. On the other hand, however, several factors can mitigate the overall impact of recessions on lawyers. While a recession may cause certain declines, individuals and corporations face other legal problems, such as bankruptcies, foreclosures, and divorces requiring legal action.

Earnings

According to the National Association for Law Placement, in 2004 the median annual earnings of lawyers nine months after graduation from law school were $55,000. Salaries varied depending on the type of work. Attorneys employed in private practice had median earnings of $80,000; those in business and industry earned $60,000. Lawyers working in judicial clerkships and government positions averaged $44,700; and those in academics earned $40,000.

The median salary for all lawyers, regardless of experience, was $94,930. The majority earned between $64,620 and $143,620. Trial lawyers generally earn more, particularly if they work in private practice. While lawyers employed by the federal government earned an average of $108,090, those working for local government (such as the city or town attorney) or state government (such as public defenders) make less, usually around $73,410 and $70,280, respectively.

Salaries of experienced attorneys vary widely according to the type, size, and location of their employer. Lawyers who own their own practices usually earn less than those who are partners in law firms, and many may need to work part-time in other occupations to supplement their income until their practice is well established.

Most salaried lawyers and judges are provided health and life insurance, and contributions are made on their behalf to retirement plans. Lawyers who practice independently are only covered if they arrange and pay for such benefits themselves.

Strategies for Finding the Jobs

The following steps are offered by attorney Gist Fleshman, whose firsthand account you read earlier in this chapter.

Work Part-Time During Law School

The best way to find a job after law school is to already have one. Many firms, government agencies, and companies with legal staff hire new attorneys who have worked for them part-time or during the summers while attending law school. This gives both sides a chance to try each other out before committing to a long-term relationship. At smaller firms with no set hiring schedule, you may well convince the firm it's time to expand.

Law School Placement Office

Your next best option is your law school's placement office, where firms and government agencies looking for attorneys with little or no experience often advertise. Some firms will come to the campus to interview prescreened applicants; ask a placement adviser about how this works at your school. Other firms simply want applicants to send them a combination of a cover letter, résumé, transcript, and writing samples. Most law schools have reciprocity with other schools' placement offices. Check with your placement director, who may have to provide a letter requesting that you be allowed to use the other school's office. This can be a valuable tool, since listings at various placement offices often differ markedly.

Ads in Legal Periodicals

Few firms advertise positions in general newspapers or magazines. Specialized legal periodicals are the place to look for job openings. For beginners, the smaller the readership, the better your chances. While you aren't likely to get one of the jobs listed in the *National Law Journal*, you do have a shot at the jobs listed in your local bar journals. Larger cities have daily legal newspapers that carry numerous ads. Call the local bar association to learn which legal periodicals cover your area.

The Internet

The Internet can be a great resource for job hunters. Many specialized periodicals that carry job postings are available online. Also, a number of websites are devoted specifically to legal positions, such as the Legal Employment Search Site at legalemploy.com. In addition to job postings, the major career sites, such as Monster.com and CareerBuilder.com, also provide useful information about résumé preparation, relocation, and other matters of interest to job seekers.

Networking

Networking may also pay dividends, and some people might even place it at the head of the list, based on their experiences. But as a new graduate, try to make sure that your network is really working for you. For example, you may know someone with enough clout to convince a law firm to interview and possibly hire you. But sometimes the interview is conducted merely as a courtesy, and the firm doesn't actually intend to consider you for a position. If this is the case, use the experience as a way of sharpening your interview skills.

The Shotgun Approach

Finally, there's the shotgun approach. You send out hundreds of letters to law firms and government agencies, simply hoping one of them will be so intrigued by you that it will set up an interview. Some people have gotten jobs this way. The reality is that unless you have a super-specialty, such as an undergraduate degree in engineering and you want to be a patent lawyer, chances are you won't get any significant responses.

One exception is applying to appellate judges. Many interview year-round for upcoming law clerk openings. Judges also tend to be poor advertisers, so the pool of applicants may be small.

Final Words of Advice

No matter what approach you take, remember these two things:

1. Send the firms and agencies exactly what they ask for. When there are 140 applicants for one opening, for example, the employer may start by automatically rejecting anyone who didn't include the requested writing sample.
2. Be careful of how you present information during interviews— complete honesty isn't always the best policy. While you certainly shouldn't lie, there are circumstances that call for reworking the truth. For example, a woman who told the interviewer that she wanted to leave her current employer because they made her work too hard. Indeed, she told the truth—to her own detriment. Although it may have been true, the employer wasn't going to hire someone who lacked the basic common sense to realize how bad that sounded to an interviewer.

Professional Associations

For information about approved law schools, bar admission requirements, and educational and career opportunities, contact the following organizations:

American Bar Association
321 North Clark St.
Chicago, IL 60610
abanet.org

Canadian Bar Association
500-865 Carling Ave.
Ottawa, ON K1S 5S8
Canada
cba.org

Federation of Law Societies of Canada
445 Boulevard Saint-Laurent, Suite 480
Montreal, QC H2Y 2Y7
Canada
flsc.ca

Information on the LSAT, the Law School Data Assembly Service, applying to law school, financial aid for law students, and law schools in the United States and Canada may be obtained from the Law School Admission Council at lsac.org.

Information on acquiring a job as a lawyer with the U.S. federal government may be obtained from the Office of Personnel Management through its website at usajobs.opm.gov. Visit jobs-emplois.gc.ca for information about working as a lawyer for the federal government of Canada.

Index